Living A Balanced Life:

A Deeper Understanding of Grace-Based Living

by

Dr. Marc A. Garcia

Living A Balanced Life:

A Deeper Understanding of Grace-Based Living

2nd Edition

Published by MBG Publishing
© 2023, Marc Garcia. All Rights Reserved
Cover design: MBG Publishing
All Scripture used is derived from King James Version unless otherwise noted.
ISBN: 978-0-9884703-6-1

Contents

Chapter 1 The Danger of Extremes   1

Chapter 2 The Scale or Balance's Construct   9

Chapter 3 Understanding Old Testament LAW   17

Chapter 4 Didn't Jesus Nullify it?   27

Chapter 5 Law Re-Defined in New Testament   39

Chapter 6 A Picture of the Balanced Life   71

To the Reader:

Welcome to the challenge I had to live and learn. Akin to my other writings this book will challenge your theology and your paradigm. I will share with you that this is not for a new believer. This book delves into the depths of the Word to discover not only the length and width of Grace but its depth and due to this a new believer may not be able to fully comprehend all that is said without a clear study of it.

None of my writings including this one have as its intent to cause confusion. The goal is to open the eyes of those who truly seek to live a grace-based life and not allow that grace to become a license to sin or license to do whatever you please. Of which we will take this journey together and discover why.

This book considers the delicate balance that should be the life of every believer in the Body of Christ. A life out of balance is a life that will give greater weight put on one principle while devaluing its counterpart.

As believers we find our society inundated with human secularism, and this has infiltrated the church like never before. This secular humanistic mindset has in my opinion watered down the effectiveness and profoundness of what HE has said in His word concerning the amazing truth of grace, and how it can co-habitate with healthy boundaries. It has also taken from the full council of the Word of God.

It has gotten to the place in many churches where Grace has been taken to an extreme to allow all types of lascivious lifestyles and support it based on the fact that Grace is in the life of the believer. The most common expression of grace has become appeasement and lack of grace has become an inability to express love. This expression of grace has robbed from the one gift God has given His creation – the true contextual understanding of what grace is and how without the reciprocal of it – diminishes the value of it.

I wrote this book not to bring condemnation but to announce a clarion call to live a balanced life. A life which understands that without a standard there is no need for grace and without grace there is no need for a standard.

The connotation of a balanced life is mentioned in scripture so many times yet goes overlooked. For example:

> [Job 31:6] **Let me be weighed in an even balance, that God may know mine integrity.**
>
> [Prov. 11:1 KJV] **A false balance [is] abomination to the LORD: but a just weight [is] his delight.**
>
> [Prov. 16:11 KJV] **A just weight and balance [are] the LORD'S: all the weights of the bag [are] his work.**
>
> [Prov. 20:23 KJV] **Divers weights [are] an abomination unto the LORD; and a false balance [is] not good.**

God uses a plumb line to show the prophet AMOS (Amos 7:7-15) that there is a standard and a balance that we are to live by. It was not something we could not achieve – it was a desired place in God's heart to have a standard by which our lives are to be balanced.

A plumb line is similar to a balance because the weight lies pointing straight down. It uses gravity to indicate balance from a central point. It will never lie – or be crooked without intervention. Where a balance uses two weights to counter each other the plumb line uses weight to show the alignment of an item based on gravity. Provided nothing is obstructing it – it will ALWAYS point straight down.

Let's jump in!

The Danger of Extremes

As human beings we tend to operate in extremes. For the most part of people's lives there is no balance between two things but mostly extreme sides.

Our democratic society is based on extremes. One side is extreme about one way and the other side is extreme on the other way. Some even call it left wing and right wing. Which is interesting that in the national bird for the U.S. is the majestic bald eagle and it needs both wings to fly.

There is an inherent danger when we operate in extremes in the Spirit. The moment we do, we begin to minimize many of the things which He has said in His word. The result is usually a "pick and choose" because it may not fit with our ideology or extreme thinking or lascivious lifestyle.

A Balanced Life

There have been many movements in the Body of Christ which have become expressed in extremes. We can think about the faith movement where all you need is faith. Although there is much truth to it, that is not "all" or "ONLY". There is the movement concerning baptism and how one must be baptized to be saved otherwise the confession is not enough; again there is some truth to that, yet it is not an "only". There is the extreme mindset now on grace, where grace handles it all. Yet again, there is some truth to that however it is not the "all".

Perhaps you have heard this before, but I want to introduce a phrase to you that I will continue to use and elaborate on in this writing and that is – "it is not either or, but both and". There are many principles that are a "both and" not an "either or".

The extreme of grace has many believing that because of grace they can do whatever they like, and all types of behaviors are accepted because grace has it covered. Some even believe that there is no need for repentance and that grace has made everyone saved.

Although my intention is not to speak ill of anyone, I do believe it is our responsibility to let the body of Christ know that this is not correct. It is the result of extreme thinking. It may even fit a sinful lifestyle. It is not our ideology or lifestyle which validates the Word, it is His Spirit. Our ideology is not the litmus test of God's word. In fact our ideology is often what He challenges to bring new revelation; new reveals of what He desires. It was always there but now the curtains are being removed to reveal it in more detail to you.

Can grace forgive you and restore you – YES! However, this cannot (and here is the danger of extremes) become a license to exercise sin or to minimize the effect of sin in the believer.

There is the mindset due to the going extreme and saying grace is above any law which states, "if I can get it past the Holy Spirit then it is ok". Yes, I have heard this spoken even by ministry leaders. However, this mentality causes an open door for a person to allow emotions and not the Word of God dictate their actions. It also bases its thought pattern that if you have accepted the Lord Jesus as your Savior then you would not do these things otherwise your conversion was not genuine. This is a fallacy which many have bought into. This thought pattern would then validate and assure us that there is NO temptation once you are saved, as well it will also dictate that there is no free-will.

The principle of free-will is not something God has or ever will compromise. You - physically - have the ability to choose what you would do when placed in "diverse temptations", you can accept what He says and believe, "fear not for I have overcome the world" OR succumb to the temptation.

We see leaders who have believed this mentality in days past fall into temptation and the results are catastrophic. Families are torn apart; people leave their dedication to the Lord simply because of an extreme thought that says, "grace covers me". There is a lack of personal and collaborative accountability which then invalidates the need for true restoration. Let's be reminded of the principle of confessing our sins one to another. (James 5:16)

As a people the Israelites tried to operate in extremes in their mentality. When they were saved from Egypt, they could not fathom that they can be free and still be chased after by their enemy. Their journey that should have taken 2-3 weeks took 40 years because of their liberal mindsets and thinking. They went to the extreme of their freedom. They also erroneously assumed that when they left there would be no enemies to try to subvert their destiny or freedom. They probably thought like many today, "I am saved and now grace takes over and any challenge to my purpose, destiny, must be against God and against His grace in my life – so I have to attack it". What if your attack was against GOD? God will often put us in situations where a challenge is presented not to thwart our purpose but to refine our growth in Him.

The Corinthians went to extremes of things as well. Their extreme was to use the "grace of God" as a license to live without restraint or dare I say to live a "lawless" existence. This created issues which the Apostle Paul had to deal with to bring clarity.

When the Corinthian church began to debate and think themselves "all that" when some said I am of Apollos, and I am of Paul and I am of Cephas (1 Corinthians 1:12) this defined an extreme for them. Their stance as an extremist was to identify themselves with a person and in turn devaluing the other – yet Paul admonishes them and says in 1 Corinthians:

> **[1 Corinthians 1:13-18] Is Christ divided? was Paul crucified for you? or were ye baptized in the name of Paul? I thank God that I baptized none of you, but Crispus and Gaius; Lest any should say that I had baptized in mine own name. And I baptized also the household of Stephanas: besides, I know not whether I baptized any other. For Christ sent me not to baptize , but to preach the gospel : not with wisdom of words, lest the cross of Christ should be made of none effect . For the preaching of the cross is to them that perish foolishness; but unto us which are saved it is the power of God. For it is written , I will destroy the wisdom of the wise, and will bring to nothing the understanding of the prudent.**

In other words he was telling them you guys are focused on who is wiser and name dropping with who you are in relationship with, when all of them (Paul, Apollos, Cephas) were teaching you about Christ and the cross. He continues to tell them (remember the Corinthians are Greek) the Jews seek signs and the Greek seek wisdom. And although this is a "both and" and not a "either or" scenario – do not lose focus because even the wisdom of man will be destroyed by the One who is wisdom – Christ.

Their extreme was dismissing the grace of God in Christ for who they "knew" and what they knew. Paul continued to debunk and separate the wisdom of God and the wisdom of the world. This was Paul's method of associating that the thought pattern was worldly wisdom not Godly wisdom. (v. 1:18-2:5)

Now relationship is important and necessary, I believe every believer should have a spiritual lineage, but that lineage does not replace the grace of God in Christ. It does not replace the relationship you have with God. It further should never even get in the way of what God tells us to do nor should the wisdom of those in relationship with you supersede the wisdom of God in His Word. If it does than you have created an idol. The Corinthians were making "wisdom by their chosen leader" their idol. A.W. Tozer so eloquently said, "an idol created by hands is as abominable to God as an idol made by an imagination or man-made wisdom".

Again, wisdom is IMPORTANT, and so are SIGNS (signs and wonders shall follow...) yet it does not stop there! It is a "both and", and not "either or".

It is my belief that many denominations have their truths and qualities that we as a people who hold on to Martin Luther's Thesis as a backbone to our faith, can use because it is not a "either or", but "both and". Even when looking at Martin Luther as a man and how his "natural" wisdom could be "mixed in" with his emotions could lead to extremes.

We as human beings seek relationships and often times even seek an idol. We would never say it, but when we speak of and dialogue about our relationship with God, we often find ourselves liking what someone may say – especially when others seem to like it as well. Yet we never take the time to study it out for ourselves to truly test the word and revelation to find validity.

As a result, this has given life to lazy Christians who take the preachers word for it, because (again we would never say it but...) we are seeking an idol.

This is never truer than in my Hispanic culture. Most Hispanics come from a Roman-Catholic upbringing. Some very devout, others (like my family) would go to mass once every 2 years. The level of devotion was superficial. However, we were taught to respect the church, believe in God, and most of all honor the Priest as God Himself, after all He like Jesus has the ability to forgive sin. It is the latter which has crept into the "Protestant Church" (Pentecostal, Baptist, Holiness – etc) because we as Hispanics brought along that honor the priest as God Himself and often times have placed church leadership at the same level of the Priest or God (again we would never say it but...)

Please do not misinterpret what I am saying. Honor is honor and give honor to whom it is due. Pray for our church leaders both Protestant and Roman-Catholic, yet there is the need for balance. We honor them not idolize them.

So let's be clear as to what an idol is. First Webster's definition of an idol is an image or other material object representing a deity to which religious worship is addressed. The Bible word for Idol is translated to be false gods. When we allow ourselves to worship false gods as God – replacing Him out of the relationship – we place ourselves at the subjection of that false god. That means the way that false god treats you, works with you, how you treat him/her, etc. will dictate your relationship and perception of your relationship with the True God!

There is a reason why God says that He is a jealous God.

> **[Exodus 20:5]: Thou shalt not bow down thyself to them, nor serve them: for I the LORD thy God am a jealous God, visiting the iniquity of the fathers upon the children unto the third and fourth generation of them that hate me;**
>
> **[Exodus 34:14]: For thou shalt worship no other god: for the LORD, whose name is Jealous, is a jealous God.**

I felt to share this portion about idols because this is 1 key item where there is a clear imbalance. I believe this one is an ONLY not both and. There is no balance act of idols and God. He even allows himself to be called JEALOUS. His name the Great "I AM" is also called Jealous.

What has occurred is we, in the use of extremes have allowed grace to replace the God who gives it. Yes grace has become an idol. It has become the thing we worship to excuse a lifestyle with no boundaries or restraints.

There are other items which are to be balanced in our lives – however our service, devotion, love, desire can be shared with nobody other than God himself. There is no scale for this – there is no both and for this – this is either or.

Moments to Ponder:

1. What are some extremes you may notice in your own life and/or walk in Christ?

2. What actions can you start to take to get balance in those areas?

A Balanced Life

The Scale or Balance's Construct

For many principles in scripture, like in science and math; on the earth – there is something called "reciprocal". It is essentially a "counterpart".

The definition of reciprocal is something that is reciprocal to something else; equivalent; counterpart; complementary.

Every created thing and every object under the sun, in the heavens has a reciprocal. It is this which creates a perfect balance on earth to sustain life.

At the sake of becoming "geeky" – Earth in itself and God's design has reciprocal seasons. Such as Winter and Summer; Fall and Spring, each have their value in the entire system. It is this system in perfect balance that helps create a planet that is habitable.

When we look at the very basics of our faith walk there are

A Balanced Life

reciprocals or counterparts to many principles. Life and death; light and darkness; hope and despair; etc.

When I speak of a balanced life – I am referring to looking at your life and see some principles through the view of a scale or "balance". From the view of a see-saw to the scale of justice where the blindfolded woman depicting justice is blind.

A balance requires two items or "weights" on each side to "counter-weight" the opposite side. If one weighs more than the other, then the balance is said to be "out of balance". In which case an adjustment must be made to one side to counter the weight or "reciprocate" the weight on the other. The result is then a balance between the two sides indicating equality of weight to both sides and both cohabitating the scale. A constant review of our life walk with Jesus through this concept will lead you to what I call a "balanced life".

For faith to operate it needs "works" to reciprocate, correspond, or dare I say, complement. Righteousness has judgment. The scripture shows us that we are made righteous.

> **[2 Cor. 5:21] For he hath made him [to be] sin for us, who knew no sin; that we might be made the righteousness of God in him.**
>
> **[Rom. 5:19] For as by one man's disobedience many were made sinners, so by the obedience of one shall many be made righteous.**
>
> **[Luke 1:6] And they were both righteous before God, walking in all the commandments and ordinances of the Lord blameless.**

Yet later it tells us that there is such a thing as righteous judgment, which in itself can appear to be an oxymoron.

> **[John 7:24] Judge not according to the appearance but judge righteous judgment.**

[Rom. 2:5] But after thy hardness and impenitent heart treasurest up unto thyself wrath against the day of wrath and revelation of the righteous judgment of God;

[2 Thes. 1:5] [Which is] a manifest token of the righteous judgment of God, that ye may be counted worthy of the kingdom of God, for which ye also suffer:

Also in scripture it says that His judgment is unto righteousness which unless you have a grasp on this understanding would seem to be a perfect metaphor.

In both examples, in specific faith and works, I would encourage you to visualize a scale with one side having faith and the other works. They are corresponding actions of each other. When they are in balance, the manifestation of the belief which the faith and corresponding action is stretched to see will manifest itself. Too much leaning on works then it is by the sweat of your brow you are trying to do something, too much leaning on faith you will sit with your arms crossed awaiting something to happen.

In what many call the "Hall of Faith" in Hebrews chapter 11, we see all of these being testified. Abraham and Sara although they had the promise from the Lord, they could not just sit and do nothing, there was a corresponding action which needed to take place. There was also an expression of imbalance with the decision of Sara to tell Abraham to "know" Hagar which yielded Ishmael. In that situation the "works" was weighing more than the faith.

The conception and birth of our Lord and Savior; Mary received Faith however that faith needed a corresponding action – a willing heart, and nine months of carrying the Savior to give birth. Not to mention the corresponding action of Joseph to still marry her and move when prompted and most notably the grace he showed her amidst the "law" and Holy Spirit's leading. Parenthetic thought: interesting how Holy Spirit's leading violated the law of Moses.

A Balanced Life

Now we look at Grace. Grace then must have a reciprocal. A "counterweight" by which can bring balance to the life of a believer – otherwise grace (which many define as unmerited favor) can become a license to abuse our freedom in Christ. The overarching definition of unmerited favor is more of a translation of what grace is. Grace does have its merits, and to enter into God's grace there needs to be a corresponding action.

We ask then, what is that counterweight? That counterweight must still be an acting principle, something by which we as believers must hold dear to the cornerstone of our faith. If it is not and if it is something absolved, then there is no way for the scale to be balanced. It would be the equivalent of removing the counterweight entirely and it does not have a reciprocating force to counter its weight.

Many believe that the counterweight of grace is mercy – especially when we read the definition given by Wilmington's Guide to the Bible where it says, *"mercy is the act of withholding deserved punishment, while grace is the act of endowing (to provide an ability not given to others) unmerited favor."*. These are more synonymous not antonymous.

In John chapter 1 – very famous scripture – John speaks of the WORD becoming flesh. In verse 17 the following words are penned:

[John 1:17]: For the law was given by Moses, but grace and truth came by Jesus Christ.

John shares how MOSES gave the Law (we will discuss that later) but Grace & Truth came by Jesus Christ. The word truth there is not referring to something that is factual. It is referring to the truth, as taught in the Christian religion, respecting God and the execution of **his purposes** through Christ, and respecting the duties of man. (source Thayer Bible expository)

The truth spoken in John 1:17 is speaking of a way of life. A method of living where God's purposes and man's responsibility collaborate with each other to fulfill the plan of God.

There must be equilibrium in the spirit for grace, otherwise the grace will be devalued when the truth is that it is a TREASURE with uncalculated worth. You see, what you do not value you will sooner or later reject. The furtherance of this would be giving up or by default lose not by God's doing but our own. When a revelation becomes too familiar it can have the potential to destroy a person's testimony. We must value our testimony! It is the one unique, impacting, life changing, signature treasure of God's manifestation in you. Our testimony is the fingerprint of God's mercy, favor and grace in our lives. Although grace remains available to you, the choice must be made to grab hold of it, and the only way you can grab hold of it is by understanding what its reciprocal is. Knowing the counterpart will allow you to value each side as well as the center of the "scale".

Let us take a moment and speak about - The scale. Aside from having two sides, it is made up of one other part which is called the fulcrum. The fulcrum is what brings the point by which the two sides are balanced on, until a weight to "tip" the scale is placed on one side which outweighs the other side. By definition, it's the point on which a lever rests or is supported and on what it pivots.

You see this principle is what Newton spoke of when he "discovered" the 3rd law of motion. *To every action there is always an **opposed and equal reaction**: or the mutual actions of two bodies upon each other are always equal and directed to contrary parts.* This is the definition of balance: a state in which different things occur in equal or proper amounts or have an equal or proper amount of importance. Newton did not discover something all his own, he discovered a perfect design by God that can apply to most of life in the spiritual as well as the natural realm.

Lets start to define the parts of the scale so that we can then enter into the spiritual ramifications of the imbalance of the scale.

A Balanced Life

The fulcrum, where both sides of the scale leverage from is KEY. In this case as we speak about grace – the fulcrum is love; the scale which includes grace teeters on the fulcrum of Love.

The fulcrum of Love is exemplified in salvation; (John 3:16) for God so loved the world. The pinnacle of grace is defined in the act of God sending His only son for us when we did not deserve it.

> **[Ezra 9:13] And after all that is come upon us for our evil deeds, and for our great trespass, seeing that thou our God hast punished us less than our iniquities [deserve], and hast given us [such] deliverance as this;**

> **[Rom. 5:8-9] But God commendeth his love toward us, in that, while we were yet sinners, Christ died for us. Much more then, being now justified by his blood, we shall be saved from wrath through him.**

Then in the letter to the Ephesians it states:

> **[Eph. 2:8] For by grace are ye saved through faith; and that not of yourselves: [it is] the gift of God:**

Grace operates in the umbrella of love – demonstrated in the salvation experience. Which is the ultimate expression of grace. Truth as mentioned in John 1, is also mentioned in its root word reference in Ephesians chapter 4.

> **[Eph. 4:15] But speaking the truth in love, may grow up into him in all things, which is the head, [even] Christ:**

This is where the writer encourages us to speak the truth in love. This would mean for us to speak of the way we are supposed to live, purposed by God to collaborate (not cooperate) with God and fulfill His will. That stuff we are to speak in LOVE has as it's goal fulfilling the will of GOD not our own will.

May I submit something to you today for your own study? Could it be that each spiritual principle rests on a balance where

The Scale or Balance's Construct

it is a **collaboration** between God and mankind. Faith & works, righteousness, and judgment; grace and ... (no its not truth)

The center point of both sides of our scale for a balanced life of grace is LOVE. The scripture tells us that God is Love. He is the fulcrum and is it on this character trait of God which hangs the balance! I believe that Love is also the fulcrum for the other "balances"; the fulcrum of the balance of faith and works is LOVE; righteousness and judgment - Love!

Since we recognize that Christ is the manifestation of grace in this earth then we must then recognize that the reason Father gave us this gift of grace was because of LOVE.

Moments to Ponder:

Take a moment and annotate each part of the scale or balance as you have learned so far.

Understanding Old Testament Law

I know, I know I said a curse word, LAW. However, let me set the scriptural base so we can continue to perhaps renew our mind concerning the "Law".

First was Adam, he had kids. Many think the only ones were Cain and Able – however there was another named Seth. Then Seth had a son Enos. Enos had Cainan; then Mahalaleel, Jared, Enoch, Methuselah, Lamech and then Moses. More than 6000 years of history – the only one documented to have a deep relationship with God was Enoch as he was taken up at the ripe age of 365. To many others this was his prime. Between Enoch and Noah approx. 1700 years pass. (Reference: Genesis 5 and Luke 3)

In Genesis chapter 6 verse 8 there seems to be a little droplet of a balanced life shown, yet it has gone unnoticed by so many. It reads,

A Balanced Life

[Gen. 6:8] But Noah found grace in the eyes of the LORD.

After God evaluates the situation and repents for creation – He looks to Noah and **sees** grace.

We have to share this to comprehend that grace came via dedication to God. A deep relationship and communication with the creator.

In Genesis chapter 6 verse 22 it says;

[Gen. 6:22] Thus did Noah; according to all that God commanded him, so did he.

The word commanded is the Hebrew word "*sava*" which was also translated to charge. So God **charged him** with the instructions to build the Ark.

The flood occurs, the waters recede, and we then find the first family lead by Noah with a ship filled with animals. In Genesis 8 here are the first things that occur:

[Gen. 8:15-21] And God spake unto Noah, saying, Go forth of the ark, thou, and thy wife, and thy sons, and thy sons' wives with thee. Bring forth with thee every living thing that [is] with thee, of all flesh, [both] of fowl, and of cattle, and of every creeping thing that creepeth upon the earth; that they may breed abundantly in the earth, and be fruitful, and multiply upon the earth. And Noah went forth, and his sons, and his wife, and his sons' wives with him: Every beast, every creeping thing, and every fowl, [and] whatsoever creepeth upon the earth, after their kinds, went forth out of the ark. And Noah builded an altar unto the LORD; and took of every clean beast, and of every clean fowl, and offered burnt offerings on the altar. And the LORD smelled a sweet savour; and the LORD said in his heart, I will not again curse the ground any more for man's sake; for the imagination of man's heart [is] evil from his youth; neither will I again smite any more every thing living, as I have done.

Verse 20 is KEY – because Noah builds an altar and brings from every clean beast, fowl and offered it as an offering to God it resulted in a sweet fragrance in the nostrils of God. Obedience has a scent.

Why is this key? Who taught him? Who told Noah about this way of honoring a God that is unseen but heard? Lets look at another example.

> **[Gen. 26:1-5] And there was a famine in the land, beside the first famine that was in the days of Abraham. And Isaac went unto Abimelech king of the Philistines unto Gerar. And the LORD appeared unto him, and said, Go not down into Egypt; dwell in the land which I shall tell thee of: Sojourn in this land, and I will be with thee, and will bless thee; for unto thee, and unto thy seed, I will give all these countries, and I will perform the oath which I sware unto Abraham thy father; And I will make thy seed to multiply as the stars of heaven, and will give unto thy seed all these countries; and in thy seed shall all the nations of the earth be blessed; Because that Abraham obeyed my voice, and kept my charge, my commandments, my statutes, and my laws.**

Verse 5 is very important to comprehend before moving on. Essentially this was a conversation between God and Isaac. What had happened is that there was famine in the land and Isaac went to King Abimelech to (we can safely assume) ask for help. On the way Yahweh speaks to him (Isaac) and tells him do not go to Egypt but go to the land which He is going to show him. God continues to tell Isaac that He will bless him and be with him, and even his children. Then now let's review what He says in verse 5 to Isaac again; **Because that Abraham obeyed my voice, kept my charge, my commandments, my statues and my laws.**

Now I know that scriptures in the KJV are not in chronological order however Genesis is the beginning. Here, way before Moses, way before Israel's slavery, the word commandment and law is used. This is

A Balanced Life

what is called in "theological circles" the "law" of first mention.

You see the majority of believers believe that the Law of Moses and the Law of God are one in the same. This thought goes further to say that since they are in the Old Testament they (Law of God and Law of Moses) are no longer in play. This has stemmed from incomplete teaching. If I may be blunt, lazy teaching, where no deeper study was done to comprehend the difference. However, we will see that this statement made to Isaac mentions 4 specific items aside from the Lord's voice these are: charge, commandments, statues, and laws.

The word charge is the Hebrew word *"mismeret"* which is translated in this context as call or injunction. So God was saying that Abraham kept his calling his function on earth. The thing he was set apart for – Abraham kept (fulfilled).

The Hebrew word there used for Commandments is *"Mitsvah"*, where traditional Jews gets "Bar-Mitsvah" or "bat-Mitsvah". This is the celebration of a young child into his/her right of passage to manhood or womanhood. In my book, He Said Follow Me, I go into detail of this celebration and its significance. In this context as bar-mitsvah is son of the law it is referring to the laws of God (as a New Testament believer).

Then the Hebrew word used for Statues is *"chuqqah"* which means ordinance. Which is a regulation declared, as in a command given from a general to a soldier. In it was direction, and process for the "soldier" to do; a S.O.P. (Standard Operating Procedure).

The term "laws" is the Hebrew word *"Torah"*. In Judaism this same word is used to collectively refer to the first 5 books of the traditional bible; Genesis – Exodus – Leviticus – Numbers – Deuteronomy. These are instructions not a mandate just simple instructions. As well because the "collective" Torah did not exist then, this now requires us to go deeper.

The *"Torah"* was not written during the time of Isaac. Nor was God's Laws (*mitsvah*) So what does it truly mean?

This is most interesting to me; the commentator Nachmanides (Ramban) explains these verses this way. It is worth noting that all other commentaries never delve into this verse like this commentator has.

"My charge is faith in Divinity – Isaac believed in the unique, and only God and kept His charge in his heart and differed from idolaters.

My Commandments includes all that He just commanded Isaac to do (instruction) 'Go forth from your land...'

My Ordinances is going in the ways of God, to be graceful and merciful and to do righteous and justice, and to command his children and his household.

My laws is the circumcision (old testament) on himself and on his children and all of the commandments of the children of NOAH as they are the law to them"

In Hebrews 11:5 references another Old Testament person who evidently pleased God, but how he did is worth noting.

[Heb. 11:5] By faith Enoch was translated that he should not see death; and was not found, because God had translated him: for before his translation he had this testimony, that he pleased God.

It is said about Enoch that He pleased God. So how can these men please God and know the **commandments**, and the **laws**, when as far as we know they did not exist? How can Enoch a descendant of Adam please God when there was no way defined for him to please God? The standard (according to many) had not been set yet.

Now what does the fact that these items are separate (law, commandments, ordinances and charge) mean to us? This means that the "thing" most charismatic churches refer to as the law now must be re-evaluated. Furthermore, this also requires that we now must understand that this is way before Moses was on the scene and spoke the ten commandments and gave the Levitical law, also known as the

A Balanced Life

Law of Moses. There is no "documented" reference to the Levitical procedures, the sacrificial standards however they knew what to do. Most scholars believe that the books where penned by Moses himself while God dictated it to him except for the last versus of Deuteronomy which is Moses' death.

Yet where did Cain and Abel learn how to give a sacrifice? How can God call one out on a standard if the standard was never defined?

So let's redefine our understanding of the New Testament believers' version of law. Law is Torah, different from Mitsvah and different from Chuqqah or a charge.

Based on this understanding we now must look at what we call the Mosaic law and God's Law differently. With this understanding we can now see that the Mosaic law which where Chuqquah aka ordinances or statues. Yet we must look into what is happening with God's Law. What does God's law refer to?

In Exodus Moses has a conversation with God before the Lord gives him the "Ten Commandments" and the other statutes; here is the dialogue:

> **[Exodus 16:28-30] And the LORD said unto Moses, How long refuse ye to keep my commandments and my laws? See , for that the LORD hath given you the sabbath, therefore he giveth you on the sixth day the bread of two days; abide ye every man in his place, let no man go out of his place on the seventh day. So the people rested on the seventh day.**

Note the reference of keeping the Shabbat or Sabbath. In verse 28 specifically the Lord speaks to Moses directly and asks him, "How long are you going to refuse to keep my commandments and my laws?" The Hebrew word for commandments there is Mitsvah and the Hebrew word for laws is Torah.

Most people, and theologians believe that the commandments and the laws where not present until Exodus 20. Yet here God is holding

Moses accountable to them. How can God hold him accountable for something he does not know of yet? Also remember Moses is the one penning these words. This is firsthand or dare I say, "from the horse's mouth".

The primary reason is because these laws and commandments were not new when presented to the people in Exodus 20, they were not being practiced mostly because the people where in slavery. How can they practice the Sabbath when they are told when to eat, sleep and work every day of their lives and disobeying that could be their entire demise? They were in slavery – subject to the rule of those who owned them.

These were observed by Abraham and Noah – verified out of the mouth of God. Yet the time gap between Noah and Moses was riddled with wars and slavery.

I believe Moses knew of them because of his "training" period in Midian with the high priest Jethro who became his father in love. He may also have known them being raised by "God's divine intervention" his mother who was an Israelite, as she served in the house of Pharoah. The latter being the most unlikely due to the limitations and generations of slavery. As well worth noting is the fact that where he was given the Ten Commandments was very close to where he experienced the burning bush experience (read Exodus 3)

Now most charismatic believers believe that the Mosaic law and the Ten Commandments comprise what we as New Testament believers collectively refer to as "the Law". Yet to group all expressions of the LAW together is not only incorrect hermeneutics but (frankly) lazy sword study..

The scriptures say consistently that He is not a liar (Num. 23:9), nor does He change (Psalms 55:9a). It tells us that His words are flawless (Prov. 30:5).

Let's create more separation between these 4 items mentioned. In Exodus is where most reference the 10 Commandments being given

A Balanced Life

to Moses. First, we must note context – this is AFTER the Israelites deliverance from Egypt, AFTER Moses fleeing to Midian and then coming back, and most of all AFTER the circling in the desert when a trip that should have taken weeks turned into years.

> **[Exodus 20:1-6] And God spake all these words, saying ,I am the LORD thy God, which have brought thee out of the land of Egypt, out of the house of bondage. Thou shalt have no other gods before me. Thou shalt not make unto thee any graven image, or any likeness of any thing that is in heaven above, or that is in the earth beneath, or that is in the water under the earth: Thou shalt not bow down thyself to them, nor serve them: for I the LORD thy God am a jealous God, visiting the iniquity of the fathers upon the children unto the third and fourth generation of them that hate me; And shewing mercy unto thousands of them that love me, and keep my commandments.**

Focus on verse 6. In the midst of Him giving the commandments to Moses he says something echoed again in Deut. 5:10 when the people of Israel needed to be reminded of the Ten Commandments anew. Then in the New Testament the words of our Savior echoes the words of the Father as God incarnate on earth.

> **[John 14:15] If ye love me, keep my commandments.**

> **[Deut. 5:10] And shewing mercy** *(hesed in Hebrew meaning in context goodness, kindness, faithfulness)* **unto thousands of them that love me and keep my commandments.**

Deut. 5:10 God speaking; John 14:15 God speaking AGAIN via Jesus.

Note – a reference to the fulcrum of the scale – Love. The 10 Commandments is later referred to as God's law versus Mosaic Law.

The Mosaic law which included all of the rituals was designed for order and tutelage for a new young, spiritual immature nation. This Law spoken of here is the Mosaic Law to instruct the new "child" in

Israel in the statutes and ordinances. It was also a setup for the coming Messiah. You see it is these statutes and ordinances where we see the types and shadows of Jesus the Messiah. It is these statutes and ordinances He came to fulfill and complete as the Lamb of God, and the last Adam. The Mosaic Law was more of a "standard operations procedure" for a new nation preparing for something later.

The Mosaic Law and the institution of it is an excellent type and shadow of a parent today. We as parents have set healthy age-appropriate boundaries for our children which define an expected conduct while under our "tutelage"; God did the same with His creation. Yet there comes a time where the child is no longer a child but an adult. It is later referred to as the schoolmaster by Apostle Paul.

[Gal. 3:24-25] Wherefore the law was our schoolmaster [to bring us] unto Christ, that we might be justified by faith. But after that faith is come, we are no longer under a schoolmaster.

The Ten Commandments are the protocol of our relationship with God. The Law of Moses is the protocol for relationships on earth and requirements of restoration if any are broken – PRIOR to the arrival and sacrifice of the Messiah.

My challenge with those who do not understand this is, if the Ten Commandments are no longer in place, then does that give me then the right as a believer to covet my neighbors' belongings? Most say if you love someone you won't do that. Well then where is the standard for Love defined? How do I know how that Love is supposed to look like, where is it in the Bible that God places it to show us? Jesus - Absolutely!

Am I not supposed to love my God with all my heart, soul and mind anymore because I am a New Testament believer? After all God told Moses, those who love me keep my commandments and statutes.

Now just like Noah we find that Moses, a murderer, a stutterer, a

A Balanced Life

leader with fits of anger finds grace in the eyes of God.

> [Exodus 33:17] And the LORD said unto Moses, I will do this thing also that thou hast spoken: for thou hast found grace in my sight, and I know thee by name.

Moses' obedience and leadership of the people (although flawed) allowed God to see GRACE in his sight. The knowing Moses by name is an indication of relationship; friendship; communication. These are pillars to how grace is seen.

Ok so here it is; no more beating around the bush or dancing around it. We have the foundation set now let's build upon it. The reciprocal of grace or the opposite side in the balanced life for grace is **God's law**. Now when I use the word "law" I am not speaking of the Mosaic Law (Levitical rituals) but more the Ten Commandments.

in summary - the balance is made up of Love being the fulcrum, on either side (you choose) there is Grace and the other side is God's law.

Moments to Ponder:

1. As per what we have learned, what are the four items that are spoken of and interpreted into law?

2. Complete the image of the balance by labeling each part of it. (Go back to the end of Chapter 2)

Didn't Jesus Nullify it?

Before moving forward, we have to now deal with the elephant in the "book". The type and shadow of the Levitical law and how Jesus fulfilled this law so that we would be saved through him and no longer have to provide a calf or a bull as a sacrifice. Nor have someone go before God on our behalf.

Now there are 603 laws in the Mosaic law – which of courase do not include the Ten Commandments. Many scholars include them together which is the primary reason why we have a theology which collects them together as one. This being said, to go through every single one and give the type and shadow of Jesus is beyond the scope of this book, not to mention it would become a commentary.

The Mosaic law I speak of includes the Levitical law. The laws tied to the priesthood and how the people of Israel had to adhere to these rules

A Balanced Life

with the goal of all becoming a royal priesthood and a chosen nation.

Galatians 3 speaks about the purpose of the law. However, a deeper understanding of this in context will reveal that this law being referred to in Galatians is NOT the Ten Commandments but the Levitical law and rituals or ordinances.

> **[Galatians 3:1] O foolish Galatians, who hath bewitched you, that ye should not obey the truth, before whose eyes Jesus Christ hath been evidently set forth, crucified among you?**

In other words what is being said is, "someone has fooled you into thinking that you do not need to obey OR BELIEVE the truth of Christ crucified.

> **[Galatians 3:2-3] This only would I learn of you, Received ye the Spirit by the works of the law, or by the hearing of faith? Are ye so foolish? having begun in the Spirit, are ye now made perfect by the flesh?**

Are you so deceived to think that you received the person of the Holy spirit because of your obedience to the works of the law (Mosaic & Levitical law). You all started in the Spirit of TRUTH – are you telling me that you were made perfect by the works of your flesh – the observance of the Mosaic and Levitical laws?

> **[Galatians 3:4-5] Have ye suffered so many things in vain? if [it be] yet in vain. He therefore that ministereth to you the Spirit, and worketh miracles among you, [doeth he it] by the works of the law, or by the hearing of faith?**

We summarize: Are you telling me that those who work miracles do so because they obey the Mosaic and Levitical laws or the ordinances placed by other church leaders or is it by faith?

> **[Galatians 3:6-7] Even as Abraham believed God, and it was accounted to him for righteousness. Know ye therefore that they which are of faith, the same are the children of Abraham.**

Remember Abraham, He obeyed (Genesis 26:5 – kept my charge, my commandments, my statutes, and my laws) this was counted to him as righteousness – very much before any ordinance the Galatians could hear of.

> **[Galatians 3:8-10] And the scripture, foreseeing that God would justify the heathen through faith, preached before the gospel unto Abraham, [saying], In thee shall all nations be blessed. So then they which be of faith are blessed with faithful Abraham. For as many as are of the works of the law are under the curse: for it is written, Cursed [is] every one that continueth not in all things which are written in the book of the law to do them.**

This is referring to Deut. 27:26 which is after the delineation of the Mosaic Law.

> **[Galatians 3:11-13] But that no man is justified by the law in the sight of God, [it is] evident: for, The just shall live by faith. And the law is not of faith: but, The man that doeth them shall live in them. Christ hath redeemed us from the curse of the law, being made a curse for us: for it is written, Cursed [is] every one that hangeth on a tree:**

This is SO powerful for those who can see it. Paul confronts the Galatians who were convinced that the observance of the Mosaic law is required. He confronts that but here in verses 12-13 of Galatians 3, Paul sums this concept up for them as an attorney builds his closing arguments.

The heathen were justified through faith based on what Abraham was told and observed. But those yes in the day – those who did not observe them were cursed, however no man is justified by the law in the sight of God. The law has no faith involved it is all flesh or dare I say works. Here it is… CHRIST redeemed us from the curse being made a curse. Christ redeemed us from the curse mentioned in Deut. 27:26. We are crucified with Christ. We are redeemed from the curse of the

A Balanced Life

Mosaic law. The Ten Commandments do not have a curse tied to it. In fact, the Hebrew word for curse is "arar" (Strongs 168) there is no use of this word or a derivative in the entire book of Exodus.

> **[Galatians 3:14] That the blessing of Abraham might come on the Gentiles through Jesus Christ; that we might receive the promise of the Spirit through faith.**

You Gentiles can therefore receive the blessing that was unto Abraham not by the Mosaic, Levitical law or rituals but your faith in the one who redeemed you on the cross. The One we are crucified with.

> **[Galatians 3:15-16] Brethren, I speak after the manner of men; Though [it be] but a man's covenant, yet [if it be] confirmed, no man disannulleth, or addeth thereto. Now to Abraham and his seed were the promises made. He saith not, And to seeds, as of many; but as of one, And to thy seed, which is Christ.**

Christ's seed is us – you and I! We are the Messiah's seed.

> **[Galatians 3:17-18] And this I say, [that] the covenant, that was confirmed before of God in Christ, the law, which was four hundred and thirty years after, cannot <u>disannul</u>, that it should make the promise of none effect. For if the inheritance [be] of the law, [it is] no more of promise: but God gave [it] to Abraham by promise.**

The covenant that was 430 years before Christ (Abrahamic covenant) cannot render void (disannul – Strongs # G208) and make the promise made via that covenant promise. It would then make the covenant useless. If the promise can be gotten by observing fleshly rituals it is no longer a promise – but a reward.

> **[Galatians 3:19-20] Wherefore then [serveth] the law? It was added because of transgressions, till the seed should come to whom the promise was made; [and it was] ordained**

> by angels in the hand of a mediator. Now a mediator is not [a mediator] of one, but God is one.

In other words serving the law is useless because then the promise would not be a promise but a reward. The Mosaic and Levitical laws were added because of transgressions or sins of man UNTIL the One who was promised by a MEDIATOR would come.

The word mediator is not referring to CHRIST it is referring to the One who MADE the promise who would mediate (strong #G3316); one who intervenes between two to restore or make peace and fellowship.

God is the mediator. He promised the One who would later come and bridge the gap between two periods of relationship.

> [Galatians 3:21-23] [Is] the law then against the promises of God? God forbid: for if there had been a law given which could have given life, verily righteousness should have been by the law. But the scripture hath concluded all under sin, that the promise by faith of Jesus Christ might be given to them that believe. But before faith came, we were kept under the law, shut up unto the faith which should afterwards be revealed.

Before Christ (faith) came we (Paul and his audience not us) were kept under the law (Mosaic and Levitical) – our faith in Christ was on pause until.

> [Galatians 3:24-29] Wherefore the law was our schoolmaster [to bring us] unto Christ, that we might be justified by faith. But after that faith is come, we are no longer under a schoolmaster. For ye are all the children of God by faith in Christ Jesus. For as many of you as have been baptized into Christ have put on Christ. There is neither Jew nor Greek, there is neither bond nor free, there is neither male nor female: for ye are all one in Christ

A Balanced Life

Jesus. And if ye [be] Christ's, then are ye Abraham's seed, and heirs according to the promise.

The Mosaic and Levitical laws were the guideposts **to** Christ. A school master is the preparation for what is to come that after growth the child understands the principle but observes it differently. Remember context – Paul is referring to the Mosaic and Levitical law that is under the curse of Deut. 27. This does not refer to the Ten Commandments.

These laws were for again the protection and establishment of a people who had never seen freedom. They needed a system of government. The Ten Commandments is not a system of civil government it is a system of KINGDOM government and relational guide.

Types and shadows are very important items when making the case and connection of Old Testament and New Testament scriptures. The word "TYPE" means "a foreshadowing; that which takes place in a natural realm pointing to the ANTITYPE (substance or reality) of the spiritual realm." Compare the Greek word "TUPOS" (Strong's #5179), which means, "a die (as struck), a stamp or scar; by analogy, a shape, a statue, (figuratively) style or resemblance; specifically, a sampler. ('type'), a model (for imitation) or instance (for warning)."

Some key types could be:

Abraham offering up his beloved son Isaac Compare: Genesis 22 with John 3:16.

The Passover Lamb – compare Exodus 12:1-23 with Matt. 26:26-28; John 1:29; 1 Cor. 5:7.

The manna from Heaven - compare Exodus 16 with John 6:48-50; 1 Cor. 10:16-17.

The smitten rock - compare Exodus 17 with 1 Cor. 10:1-4.

The nation of Israel, the Old Testament Church - compare Acts 7:38; 1 Cor. 10:1-11.

The priests Aaron and Melchisedec - compare Genesis 14; Exodus 28-29 with Heb. 5:1-8:6.

The serpent on the pole - compare Num. 21:8-9 with John 3:14.

Jonah in the fish for 3 days and 3 nights - compare Jonah 1 with Matt. 12:39-41.

These types give us an indication that there are foretelling's of what was to come. They confirm each other just like the Tabernacle or the Tent of Meeting with Moses would foretell the Messiah and what He would fulfill.

I read it from a great man of God who is no longer with us and since I cannot make it any better I will quote from his book:

"The Tabernacle of Moses is the "grandfather clause" of knowing and understanding the Holy Scriptures. ...

... The Bible is full of pictures—God uses the "show and tell" method for His children. Moses' Tabernacle is the basis of all biblical typology. The first five books of the Bible—Genesis, Exodus, Leviticus, Numbers, and Deuteronomy, which are known as the Pentateuch, the Torah, or the Law—are almost entirely typical, and many other parts of the Word of God abound with types." (Dr. Kelley Varner - Tabernacle of Moses)

Because of this fact I want to show you how Jesus is personified in the Tabernacle that God called Moses to build and even typified in the temple built by Solomon.

If we see the types and shadows in the Old Testament, we can then see the fulfillment of the same in the New Testament, or dare I say be able to separate what is fulfilled and not fulfilled.

As we have seen the "LAW" as it refers to the Old Testament can be gathered in 3 categories. They are moral (ten commandments or Torah), civil (Mosaic Law), and ceremonial (Levitical Law). These are then demonstrated in the Tabernacle, the five Offerings (Burnt, Meal,

A Balanced Life

Peace, Sin, and Trespass), the three major Feasts (Passover, Pentecost, and Tabernacles), and the Levitical Priesthood (including the high priestly garments of glory and beauty).

The only set personified in Jesus and fulfilled by Jesus is the Tabernacle, the Five Offerings, the 3 major feasts and the Levitical priesthood. Let's dive into it and see how this occurred with scriptural basis. Please note ALL of these are POST even Moses being given the Ten Commandments.

The Tabernacle in itself was not only a method of teaching the new free Israelites about their relationship with God but also give them a method by which they are to approach God. If you are to read Exodus 25-31 you will see in great detail and how detail-oriented God is with giving the Israelites these instructions.

The Hebrew word for Tabernacle is Mishkan; first mentioned in Exodus 25:9. It is translated as "dwelling place". God allowed Moses to build a dwelling place engineered by God for God himself. God the Architect – Moses the builder. (Oh look that collaboration thing again)

This relationship between the two was initiated with the giving of the Mosaic and Levitical law and continued into the construction of God's dwelling place.

The materials to be used in the construction of the tabernacle would be materials that would later give us a type of Christ. Each item in the Tabernacle gives us a complete picture of Christ as the person, Savior and Lamb of God. Jesus was at the center of God's engineering plan of the tabernacle with the goal of having Jesus as the center of our lives, ministry, marriage, etc.

If we were to take the tabernacle and form it into a 3d object and stand it upright we would see the cross. The brazen alter at His feet of brass, the lavar as his midsection and innermost emotions. The golden candle stick and the show bread are his arms outstretched. The Golden altar would be the heart of Christ, and the Ark with the 2 angels facing each other or the mercy seat being the mind of Christ.

The tribal arrangement of the camp at rest was shaped in the form of a CROSS. What we see clearly in the Tabernacle of Moses is a CROSS WITHIN A CROSS (review Deut. 21:22-23; Matt. 16:24; 27:22-26; Rom. 6:6; Gal. 2:20; 3:13-14; 5:11,24; Eph. 2:6; Col. 1:20; 2:14; Phil. 2:8; Heb. 12:2).

The outer court is the first step into the presence of God and it is a type and shadow or our elementary salvation experience. It is here in the brazen altar – Christ's feet of brass – where He is the Passover Lamb (1 cor. 5:7; Rev. 13:8) and the Lavar outside Christ is represented in the water baptism.

There is much more to discover in just the outer court, however we progress forward into the Holy Place where we find the show bread and the candle sticks. These reveal the provision of God for not just food but revelation. Light is a type and shadow of revelation. Bread is symbol of provision. **Man shall not eat of bread alone but by every word that proceeds out of the mouth of God. [Matt. 4:4 & Luke 4:4]** So there is a need for bread but also revelation. The candle sticks represent what Jesus referred to as the revelatory words from the mouth of God. This is why these two also depict his right and left arms extended (bread and candles).

As we then progress into the Holy of Holies, there is the infamous curtain which makes separation which would be torn when Jesus is crucified indicating to us that we come through the outer court, into the holy place but now we can enter the holy of holies and sit on the mercy seat. It is important to note that these curtains were one solid piece and 3 textiles thick. The tearing of these curtains give us access to the mind of Christ. (Review 1 peter 1:13; 1 Co. 2:16)

> **[Matt. 1:23; Acts 4:12; Eph. 2:14] Thou shalt call his name JESUS: for He shall save his people from their sins...Neither is there SALVATION in any other...For He is our PEACE...and hath broken down the middle wall..."**

A Balanced Life

Then we enter into the priestly duties. The duties of the priest in the time of Moses Tabernacle were deadly in some cases. Yet we can even see Christ manifested in type and shadow via persons who broke protocol for the priests. For example, King David taking on the ephod (priestly garment) to get wisdom from God concerning a turbulent situation. (1 Samuel 23:9; 1 Samuel 30:7)

The main focus of the Levitical law was the sacrifice. The method and procedure was delineated not only in the requirements of the tabernacle in the dessert but also in the Mosaic law. Yet the role of the High Priest fell on Jesus. In Hebrews 3:1; 4:14; and 6:20 the writer refers to Jesus as the High Priest to the Hebrew people living in the "Mosaic Law" by saying:

> **[Hebrews 3:1] Wherefore, holy brethren, partakers of the heavenly calling, consider the Apostle and High Priest of our profession, Christ Jesus;**
>
> **[Hebrews 4:14] Seeing then that we have a great high priest, that is passed into the heavens, Jesus the Son of God, let us hold fast [our] profession.**
>
> **[Hebrews 6:20] Whither the forerunner is for us entered, [even] Jesus, made an high priest for ever after the order of Melchisedec.**

The Lamb, the ram, the goat was type and shadow of Jesus.

He is the Lamb of God who takes away the sin of man (John 1:29,36).

He is the scapegoat which delivers us from the hands of the enemy when He was tempted for 40 days in the wilderness.

> **[Leviticus 16:8-10] He** *(Aaron – High Priest)* **is to cast sacred lots to determine which goat will be reserved as an offering to the LORD and which will carry the sins of the people to the wilderness of Azazel. Aaron will then present as a sin offering the goat chosen by lot for the LORD. The other goat, the scapegoat chosen by lot to be sent away, will be**

kept alive, standing before the LORD. When it is sent away to Azazel in the wilderness, the people will be purified and made right with the LORD.

What we begin to truly see now is how Christ is typefied in the Tabernacle, and the levitical duties. This I hope has "sparked" your appetite to search for more on your own. Yet as mentioned to go into deep detail of the 603 laws one by one is beyond the scope of this writing. I do believe this will give enough evidence to show that where **He is written of - He has fulfilled**. Once fulfilled there is no need to expect another manifestation of the same to accomplish the same - this is called singular prophetic manifestation.

God had it all covered in His engineered construct of Christ, all through out, His "show and tell" is completed in the New Testament.

Moments to Ponder:

Can you think of any other types and shadows that give clear evidence of what Christ has FULFILLED?

A Balanced Life

The ReDefinition of "Law" in the New Testament

As we continue to discover the balanced life there must be more clarity brought to Paul's writing about this topic. In the dissertation of Grace from the book of Romans there is a vast use of the word "law". It is this which has resulted in much confusion and hyper-grace in the body of Christ.

In the New Testament there are 3 primary Greek words used that are translated from law. They are *nomos*, *entole* and the 3rd is *"entalma"*. Each one because it is used in the Greek language (a descriptive language) can refer to different things when used. This means that context is extremely important. Context in new testament format letters or epistles is defined in who is the audience, the purpose of the letter, the person writing the letter and the spirit of the writing. This differs in comparison to the historical books of the Old Testament which demonstrates the importance of being a student of the Bible.

The following are some of the translations to these Greek words but again it is not a one size fits all. Entalma is important as this refers to man-made rules mentioned only 3 times in the New Testament; twice by Jesus:

> **[Mark 7:7] Howbeit in vain do they worship me, teaching for doctrines the commandments** *(entalma)* **of men.**
>
> **[Matthew 15:9] But in vain they do worship me, teaching for doctrines the commandments** *(entalma)* **of men.**

This is worth noting because Jesus made reference to man-made rules by means of vain worship and compared them to entole another word for law or commandment.

The use of the word commandment by the translator then cannot be used as a "global" definition in the New Testament. Here are some examples but keep in mind the goal is to illustrate the importance of context.

> **[Mark 7:8-9] For laying aside the commandment** *(entole)* **of God,** *(and focus on entalma)* **ye hold the tradition of men, [as] the washing of pots and cups: and many other such like things ye do. And he said unto them, Full well ye reject the commandment** *(entole)* **of God, that ye may keep your own tradition.** *(entalma)*

When many of the scriptures in the New Testament mention the word Law it is usually coupled with the Mosaic Law however when the word commandment is used it is coupled with many times the word Love. Yet there is a 3rd reference to the word law which simply means law or rule of the land/society. It is worth noting that just like our culture in the United States our laws of society are based on what many call Judeo-Christian values or the Ten Commandments.

Jesus uses the word law or commandment multiple times however He is not referencing the Mosaic law or the Ten Commandments. He

The ReDefinition of "Law" in the New Testament

is simply referring to the cultural rules. The Old Testament equivalent would be statutes or ordinances. For example, here it is translated as an order, or a command from a leader to those who are following him. It is not a new commandment we are supposed to adhere to:

[Matthew 8:18] Jesus gave the disciples "commandment" (entole) to go to the other side.

Here the word commandment would be more referring to the word charge from the old testament. This is the CALL Jesus received from the Father:

[John 10:18] No man taketh it from me, but I lay it down of myself. I have power to lay it down, and I have power to take it again. This commandment (entole) have I received of my Father.

This is why context is so important when reading, interpreting and sharing scripture. If not then these words which can be used in different methods may foster erroneous teachings and manipulation or dare I say false teaching *(not a false teacher just unsure teachings)*.

"Entole" is mentioned 65 times in the New Testament. Mentioned the most in 1 John; in 5 "chapters" it is mentioned 10 times: 1 John 2:4; 1 John 2:7-8; 1 John 3:22-24; 1 John 4:21; 1 John 5:3. "Entole" as per the context of what we are sharing here is translated as, an order, command, charge, precept, injunction.

The second Greek word for commandment is nomos, mentioned 165 times in the New Testament. 51 times alone in the book often referred to as the book of grace – Romans. "Nomos" is translated as, anything established, anything received by usage, a custom, a law.

With these two being defined then we can deduce that the comparison or equivalent between Old Testament and New Testament, as those who spoke of in the New Testament were referring to the Old Testament equivalent. Yet this does not remove the need for contextual understanding.

Hebrew (OT)	Greek (NT)	Indicative of
mismeret	entalma	Call, charge, injunction
Chuquah	Entole	Ten Commandments
Torah, Mitzvah	Nomos	Mosaic Law or customs, rule or system of rules

[Matthew 15:3-4,6] But he answered and said unto them, Why do ye also transgress the commandment (entole) of God by your tradition? *(Greek word is paradosis which is translated to mean ritual)* **For God commanded, saying, Honour thy father and mother: and, He that curseth father or mother, let him die the death. And honour not his father or his mother, [he shall be free]. Thus have ye made the commandment (entole) of God of none effect by your tradition.** *(Again paradosis = rituals)*

Compare these with the following examples of nomos in the New Testament. This will continue to reveal that when the word LAW is mentioned in the New Testament it is not ALL INCLUSIVE to Ten Commandments, Mosaic Law, Levitical law.

The book of Luke was focused to the Jewish people and in that book we can see the following within this context:

[Luke 2:22] And when the days of her purification according to the law of Moses *(nomos)* **were accomplished, they brought him to Jerusalem, to present him to the Lord.**

Law of Moses is rituals which Mary had to go through concerning Jesus (note it was not only Mary but every Jew had to adhere to these "rules"). Levitus 12 speaks of this rule in particular that for the first seven days after childbirth she is considered unclean.

Then on the 8th day she is considered restored but also this is when the male child is supposed to be circumcised. Now here is something interesting because that circumcision rule did not come AFTER the freedom of the Israelites from captivity. It was reinstituted in Genesis 17:12; as well we cannot forget when Abraham circumcised his son Isaac Gen. 21:4. This is important because it reveals to us that these things were already in place but due to the Israelites captivity were dormant.

Yet now Jesus refers to them – in particular the Mosaic law that is spoke of him and those things needed to be fulfilled and have been fulfilled. Not NULLIFIED but FULFILLED.

> **[Luke 24:44] And he said unto them, These are the words which I spake unto you, while I was yet with you, that all things must be <u>fulfilled</u>, which were written in the law of Moses** *(nomos)***, and in the prophets, and in the psalms, <u>concerning me</u>...**

If the Law of Moses and the Ten Commandments are to be all inclusive then where is Jesus mentioned in the Ten Commandments? He is not! There is no type and shadow of Jesus in the Ten Commandments. There are only types and shadows of Jesus in the fulfilling each one of the Levitical and/or Mosaic law. As well as his very presence being a fulfillment of prophetic voices.

> **[Hebrews 9:19-22] For when Moses had spoken every precept to all the people according to the law** *(nomos)***, he took the blood of calves and of goats, with water, and scarlet wool, and hyssop, and sprinkled both the book , and all the people.**

Moses' process was a type and shadow of Jesus. This was done in Exodus 24 and further explained in Lev. 16 with the subtitle "the Law of the Atonement".

> **[Acts 13:39] And by him all that believe are justified from all things, from which ye could not be justified by the law** *(nomos)* **of Moses.** *(Again if there is distinction of the law of Moses then there must be another distinction between the other "laws")*

A Balanced Life

> **[Matthew 19:17] And he said unto him, Why callest thou me good? there is none good but one, that is, God: but if thou wilt enter into life, keep the commandments** *(entole)*. **whom tribute is due; custom to whom custom; fear to whom fear; honour to whom honour.** *(Remember Matthew's recount is focused to the Jews and all of which are mentioned in the Ten Commandments of Exodus 20:1-17)*

The Apostle Paul uses nomos often, especially in the letter to the Romans. So in reading, we must understand context; audience and purpose. The Romans only new the rituals by example of the Jews. So Paul had to meet them there BUT delineate what he means. Let's discover together.

First we must realize that this writing was before Paul ever reached Rome. It was sent with Pheobe a deaconess to the mission in Rome. So – this means Paul had not been there yet. He had not had a preconceived idea based on experience with them. This was based on the limited information he knew about them.

The form of the Epistle may throw further light on the "why". The letter falls, overall, into three parts. Although for this study we will separate it into themes, keep in mind that the letter was written without chapters, versus or theme headings.

First, we have Romans 1-8 inclusive, a prolonged exposition of the contrasted and related phenomena of sin and salvation, with special initial references to the cases of Jew and non-Jew respectively.

Second, comes Romans 9-11, which deal with the Jewish rejection of the Jewish Messiah.

Lastly we have Romans 12-16. Some account of the writer's plans, and his salutations to friends, requests for prayer, etc., form the close of this section. But it is mainly a statement of Christian duty in common life, personal, civil, religious. *(Source in part: International*

The ReDefinition of "Law" in the New Testament

Standard Bible Encyclopedia)

The heterogeneous composition of this church (the Roman Church) explains the general character of the Epistle to the Romans. It was: therefore, the business of the Christian teacher to reconcile the opposing difficulties and to hold out a meeting-point in the gospel. This is exactly what Paul does in this letter to them.

Now let me prepare you for what is about to happen. We are going to go into an in-depth bible study of scripture as it pertains to how the Apostle Paul uses the word "law" and we will build a case with clarity that it is not ALL referring to the collective of "the law" (Mosaic Law, God's Law, Rituals, Levitical Law, Customs). With this in mind take your time – read and study the scriptures and the commentary I provide.

These first 8 chapters as previously mentioned are an exposition of the contrast of sin and salvation. Or dare we saw Law and Grace with love as its fulcrum for the context of our discussion.

The church in Rome were not novices and Paul speaks to them about key principles even in the beginning of the letter. Starting with the cornerstone statement of our faith today – The Just shall live by faith. Then he deals with such items as the wrath of unrighteousness and topics like adultery, homosexuality, an abased mind, lust, etc. (Romans 1:16-32)

As we continue the letter, (aka chapter 2) Apostle Paul introduces context and explains in verse 11 and 12; then continues through verse 16 and beyond. Let's first expand on this part:

> **[Romans 2:11-16 NKJV] For there is no partiality with God. For as many as have sinned without law will also perish without law, and as many as have sinned in the law will be judged by the law (for not the hearers of the law [are] just in the sight of God, but the doers of the law will be justified; for when Gentiles, who do not have the law, by nature do the things in the law, these, although not having**

> the law, are a law to themselves, who show the work of the law written in their hearts, their conscience also bearing witness, and between themselves [their] thoughts accusing or else excusing [them]) in the day when God will judge the secrets of men by Jesus Christ, according to my gospel.

For there is no partiality (or respect of persons) in God. Now many use this in the context of, "if it happened for someone else it can happen for me" however the context is that God will judge each according to their deeds (verse 6). This has nothing to do with blessings or even favor but judgment. Think about that next time you want to use that scripture out of context. No judgment – many of us have done it and perpetuated it as preachers – but now...

Next he introduces the word *nomos* (law) into the conversation of the letter. He essentially says, those who sinned without the nomos (Gentiles) will also perish without the nomos. Likewise those who have the law (the Jews) will also perish with the law (*nomos*). He makes a clear declaration that regardless of the nomos we all are going to die regardless of being jew or gentile. As a student (Berean) of the word we must also note that the translator felt it necessary to include the following as a parenthetic thought.

> **[verses 13-15] (for not the hearers of the law [are] just in the sight of God, but the doers of the law will be justified; for when Gentiles, who do not have the law, by nature do the things in the law, these, although not having the law, are a law to themselves, who show the work of the law written in their hearts, their conscience also bearing witness, and between themselves [their] thoughts accusing or else excusing [them])**

Without the parenthetic thought the scripture would read:

> **[Romans 2:11-12, 16 NKJV] For there is no partiality with God. For as many as have sinned without law will also perish without law, and as many as have sinned in the law**

The ReDefinition of "Law" in the New Testament

will be judged by the law in the day when God will judge the secrets of men by Jesus Christ, according to my gospel.

You see the reality is that whether you know the Lord as Savior or not there is a law you operate in. That law is in either witnessing to the mind or excusing it to the mind – Paul uses the word thoughts.

[2 Corinthians 10:2-4 NKJV] For though we walk in the flesh, we do not war after the flesh: (For the weapons of our warfare [are] not carnal, but mighty through God to the pulling down of strong holds;) Casting down imaginations, and every high thing that exalteth itself against the knowledge of God, and bringing into captivity every thought to the obedience of Christ;

Note the word imaginations. This is part of your mind or soul. If you recall we are a Spirit, we live in a body (flesh) and we have a soul (mind, will, intellect).

I want to repeat this because you have to have this in mind as we delve deeper into Romans. We are a Spirit, we live in a body (flesh) and we have a soul (mind, will, intellect).

In my book "Prosperity Delusion" I speak about the prosperity of each of these as part of the 5 areas of life God wants us to prosper in. So, we are even more clear I am not speaking SOLELY of money when I use the word prosper. Prosper by definition is flourish physically; grow strong and healthy and in my book Prosperity Delusion I go much deeper into this.

As we continue in our study of Romans let us again remind ourselves of the following KEY points:

We are a Spirit, we live in a body (flesh) and we have a soul (mind, will, intellect).

Romans 2:17-29 Paul confronts the Jew and when using the word law primarily reflects on the Mosaic law but uses the word law in the context of rules as well. For the Jew the Law of Moses is their cornerstone. However again these were converted Jews who Paul tries to reach them with their foundational understanding to help them grow in faith in Christ. Please note that this will include expansion and original Greek word expounding as we study the epistle of Romans.

> **[Romans 2:17-29 NKJV] Indeed you are called a Jew, and rest on the law, and make your boast in God, and know [His] will, and approve the things that are excellent, being instructed out of the law** *(nomos and in another scripture is referenced as the Pedagogos or tutor)*, **and are confident that you yourself are a guide to the blind, a light to those who are in darkness, an instructor of the foolish, a teacher of babes, having the form of knowledge and truth in the law** *(nomos)*. **You, therefore, who teach another, do you not teach yourself? You who preach that a man should not steal, do you steal?** *(here is the reference to the Law of Moses AS well as the commandments)* **You who say, "Do not commit adultery," do you commit adultery? You who abhor idols, do you rob temples? You who make your boast in the law** *(nomos)*, **do you dishonor God through breaking the law** *(nomos)*? **For "the name of God is blasphemed among the Gentiles because of you," as it is written. For circumcision is indeed profitable if you keep the law** *(nomos)*; **but if you are a breaker of the law** *(nomos)*, **your circumcision has become uncircumcision. Therefore, if an uncircumcised man keeps the righteous requirements of the law** *(nomos)*, **will not his uncircumcision be counted as circumcision?** *(Circumcision is a requirement of the Mosaic law)* **And will not the physically uncircumcised, if he fulfills the law** *(nomos)*, **judge you who, [even] with [your] written [code]** *(actually original word is law or nomos calling them out on their man mad law)* **and circumcision, [are] a transgressor of the law** *(nomos)*? **For he is not a Jew who [is one] outwardly, nor [is] circumcision that which [is] outward**

The ReDefinition of "Law" in the New Testament

> in the flesh; but [he is] a Jew who [is one] inwardly; and circumcision [is that] of the heart, in the Spirit, not in the letter; whose praise [is] not from men but from God.

The Apostle Paul speaks to them about how their outward appearance means nothing. Remember Spirit, Soul, Flesh. He admonishes them to get circumcised in the SPIRIT not the flesh.

Romans 3 continues but segues to another point Paul wants to make. Remember chapters and verses are there for the translator, I am trying to make this just like Paul wrote it – without the chapters and verse separations.

He begins with a rhetorical question then answers it:

> [Romans 3:1-5 NKJV] What advantage then has the Jew, or what [is] the profit of circumcision? Much in every way! Chiefly because to them were committed the oracles of God. *(The Apostle Paul does concede favor to the Jews here for being the oracles of God, the one's who paved the way for God's manifestation in Jesus – he honors them for their part in that)* For what if some did not believe? Will their unbelief make the faithfulness of God without effect? Certainly not! Indeed, let God be true but every man a liar. As it is written: "That You may be justified in Your words, And may overcome when You are judged." But if our unrighteousness demonstrates the righteousness of God, what shall we say? [Is] God unjust who inflicts wrath?

(Paul refers to himself as a man but not the gender but the species and that of a "fallen" species.)

> [Romans 3:6-7 NKJV] Certainly not! For then how will God judge the world? For if the truth of God has increased through my lie to His glory, why am I also still judged as a sinner? *(again he referred to himself as a fallen man previously he is no longer a sinner – a person who practices sin and without a covenant)*

A Balanced Life

[Romans 3:8-9 NKJV] And [why] not [say], "Let us do evil that good may come"?--as we are slanderously reported and as some affirm that we say. Their condemnation is just. What then? Are we better [than they]? Not at all. For we have previously charged both Jews *(covenant)* **and Greeks** *(non- covenant)* **that they are all under sin.** *(Fallen state without Christ)*

[Romans 3:10-31 NKJV] As it is written: "There is none righteous, no, not one; *(often times used to fortify the thought of how we are all sinners and we are not righteous but lets look at how this comes alive before our eyes)* **There is none who understands; There is none who seeks after God. They have all turned aside; They have together become unprofitable; There is none who does good, no, not one." "Their throat [is] an open tomb; With their tongues they have practiced deceit"; "The poison of asps [is] under their lips"; "Whose mouth [is] full of cursing and bitterness." "Their feet [are] swift to shed blood; Destruction and misery [are] in their ways; And the way of peace they have not known."** *(the WAY OF PEACE – Christ – they have not known)* **"There is no fear of God before their eyes."** *(no wisdom of God which yields the fear of God)* **Now we know that whatever the law says, it says to those who are under the law, that every mouth may be stopped, and all the world may become guilty before God.** *(The law yields the conviction to sin and acknowledgment of the flaws in us and a need for a Savior.)*

Therefore, by the deeds of the law no flesh will be justified in His sight, for by the law [is] the knowledge of sin. But now the righteousness of God apart from the law is revealed, being witnessed by the Law *(law of Moses)* **and the Prophets, even the righteousness of God, through faith in Jesus Christ, to all and on all who believe. For there**

The ReDefinition of "Law" in the New Testament

is no difference; for all have sinned and fall short of the glory of God, being justified freely by His grace through the redemption that is in Christ Jesus, whom God set forth [as] a propitiation by His blood, through faith, to demonstrate His righteousness, because in His forbearance God had passed over the sins that were previously committed, to demonstrate at the present time His righteousness, that He might be just and the justifier of the one who has faith in Jesus. *(The amazing work of righteousness and salvation in each of us)* **Where [is] boasting then? It is excluded. By what law** *(nomos but not referring to any Levitical or Mosaic law but precept)***? Of works? No, but by the law** *(nomos; principle)* **of faith. Therefore we conclude that a man is justified by faith apart from the deeds of the law** *(rituals or precepts)***. Or [is He] the God of the Jews only? [Is He] not also the God of the Gentiles? Yes, of the Gentiles also, since [there is] one God who will justify the circumcised by faith** *(law of Moses and covenant)* **and the uncircumcised** *(no covenant)* **through faith. Do we then make void (nullify; abolish) the law** *(nomos – but rule or principle)* **through faith? Certainly not! On the contrary, we establish** *(stand upon)* **the law** *(nomos principle of – faith as mentioned)*.

In Romans 4 he solidifies the concept of what he is sharing by giving examples. First Abraham, then David, and explains how in the same way a man would be paid for their work – salvation will not come from work but grace. The only collaborator of "works" is faith. (Faith without works is dead).

In Romans 4:9-12 there is something important we cannot glance over. Keep in mind context and how we have established a clear context for this writing. Paul shares the following with the Christian Jews and Gentiles in Rome about Abraham:

> [Romans 4:9-12 NKJV] [Does] this blessedness *(righteousness)* then [come] upon the circumcised [only], or upon the uncircumcised also? For we say that faith was accounted to Abraham for righteousness. How then was it accounted? While he was circumcised, or uncircumcised? Not while circumcised, but while uncircumcised. And he received the sign of circumcision, a seal of the righteousness of the faith which [he had while still] uncircumcised, that he might be the father of all those who believe, though they are uncircumcised, that righteousness might be imputed to them also, and the father of circumcision to those who not only [are] of the circumcision, but who also walk in the steps of the faith which our father Abraham [had while still] uncircumcised.

Remember the challenge which was posed earlier in chapter 3. The Apostle Paul is saying the same thing here. While speaking to Moses God refers to Abraham and says, **"Because that Abraham obeyed my voice, and kept my charge, my commandments, my statutes, and my laws." (Genesis 26:5)**

As Paul describes this was done BEFORE the circumcision referring to the Mosaic Law which supposedly came later but now we know did not.

It was Abraham's belief in the One who gave him these charges and commandments, and he in keeping them that made it count unto him as righteousness. This is the one God called His friend.

> [Romans 4:13-15 NKJV] *(Here the word law is most used to reference the Mosaic law.)* **For the promise that he (Abraham) would be the heir of the world [was] not to Abraham or to his seed through the law** *(rituals in this case circumcision)*, **but through the righteousness of faith. For if those who are of the law** *(nomos)* **[are] heirs (the jews), faith is made void and the promise made of no effect, because**

the law *(nomos)(practiced by the Jews)* **brings about wrath; for where there is no law [there is] no transgression.**

The keypoint here, is that without the Law there is no transgression – The word there for transgression is *parabasis* which is translated to mean a violation of the Mosaic Law. In layman's terms – if there is no law against speeding then there will never be a violation of it. There must be something to transgress for a violation to occur and retribution or redemption to be needed.

> **[Romans 4:16-18 NKJV] Therefore [it is] of faith** *(Greek word pistis which is translated to mean conviction of truth)* **that [it might be] according to grace, so that the promise might be sure to all the seed, not only to those who are of the law** *(nomos – in this case Abrahamic covenant and circumcision.)*, **but also to those who are of the faith** *(pistis – the conviction of the truth about Abraham)* **of Abraham, who is the father of us all** *(as it is written, "I have made you a father of many nations")* **in the presence of Him whom he believed - God, who gives life to the dead and calls those things which do not exist as though they did; who, contrary to hope, in hope believed, so that he became the father of many nations, according to what was spoken...**

This scripture is a GREAT example of the need to understand context and the depth of what is being said. Paul speaks of Abraham contrary to hope, in hope believed... How can one believe in hope and it be in contrary to HOPE. The Greek word used there is *"elpis"* and it was used to translate both the positive and the negative. It can mean, expectation of evil, fear, anxiety as well as expectation of good, hope. So with this in mind we can deduce that what Paul is trying to communicate is that Abraham contrary to the expectation in fear and anxiety, in the expectation of good he believed, so that he became the father. You know, how we are often pressed to believe a Word from God when everything around us seems like fulfillment is impossible – well just like that. Let us continue.

[Romans 4:18b-25 NKJV] "So shall your descendants be." And not being weak in faith *(conviction of truth)*, he did not consider his own body, already dead *(since he was about a hundred years old)*, and the deadness of Sarah's womb. He did not waver at the promise of God through unbelief, but was strengthened in faith, giving glory to God, and being fully convinced that what He had promised He was also able to perform. And therefore "it was accounted to him for righteousness." *(The "it" is the faith and hope the conviction of truth in the expectation of good)* Now it was not written for his sake alone that it was imputed *(Greek word for imputed is ellogeō translated to mean; set to one's account, lay to one's charge. The English definition of imputed is, accounted to someone by virtue of a similar quality in another)* to him, but also for us. It shall be impute to us *(accounted to us by the similar quality)* who believe in Him who raised up Jesus our Lord from the dead, who was delivered up because of our offenses *(greek: paraptoma - a lapse or deviation from truth and uprightness)*, and was raised because of our justification *(greek: dikaiosis - the act of God declaring men free from guilt and acceptable to him)*.

[Romans 5:18-Romans 6:3 NKJV] Therefore, as through one man's offense [judgment came] to all men, resulting in condemnation, even so through one Man's righteous act [the free gift came] to all men, resulting in justification of life. *(Here Paul is speaking of Adam)* For as by one man's disobedience *(Adam)* many were made sinners, so also by one Man's obedience *(Jesus)* many will be made righteous. Moreover, the law *(nomos Mosaic Law)* entered that the offense might abound. *(Greek word – pleonazō which is translated to mean to increase. Because without the law there is no transgression. to protect humanity and God's relationship with us and give value to that relationship)* But

The ReDefinition of "Law" in the New Testament

where sin *(fault or a violation of the divine law in thought or in act)* **abounded,** *(Greek word – pleonazō as above)* **grace abounded** *(Different Greek word from the other abound – this word is hyperperisseuō which means – via translation - to overflow, to enjoy abundantly. The Greek word includes a superlative word "very")* **much more, so that as sin reigned in death** *(not physical death but spiritual death)***, even so grace might reign through righteousness to eternal life** *(denotes two points of time – righteousness = moment of salvation and eternal life = once we physically die and be in His presence in heaven)* **through Jesus Christ our Lord. What shall we say then? Shall we continue in sin that grace may abound? Certainly not! How shall we who died to sin live any longer in it? Or do you not know that as many of us as were baptized into Christ Jesus were baptized into His death? Therefore, we were buried with Him through baptism into death, that just as Christ was raised from the dead by the glory of the Father, even so we also should walk in newness of life. For if we have been united together in the likeness of His death, certainly we also shall be [in the likeness] of [His] resurrection, knowing this, that our old man** *(sinful nature or flesh)* **was crucified with [Him], that the body of sin** *(body of sin = flesh)* **might be done away with, that we should no longer be slaves of sin** *(fault caused by the choices of our flesh or old man)***. For he who has died has been freed from sin. Now if we died with Christ, we believe that we shall also live with Him, knowing that Christ, having been raised from the dead, dies no more.**

Keynote: This is NOT speaking of his physical death, remember above Paul spoke of how in baptism he died and rose again – the context continues here. We continue...

Death no longer has dominion over Him. For [the death] that He died *(in baptism)***, He died to sin once for all; but**

> **[the life] that He lives** *(post baptism)*, **He lives to God. Likewise, you also, reckon yourselves to be dead indeed to sin** *(Once forever)*, **but alive to God in Christ Jesus our Lord. Therefore, do not let sin reign in your mortal body** *(flesh)*, **that you should obey it in its lusts** *(as if it was never put to death)*. **And do not present your members [as] instruments of unrighteousness to sin but present yourselves to God as being alive from the dead, and your members [as] instruments of righteousness to God. For sin shall not have dominion over you, for you are not under law but under grace.**

This statement cannot stand alone; the word for in the beginning denotes in Greek a conjunction it is better to see this as THEREFORE to help understand the context. Here is perhaps a more accurate interpretation of that: So as our members are instruments of righteousness, therefore sin shall not have dominion over you, because your members are instruments of righteousness you are not under the law but under grace then it continues...

As we just saw in chapter 5 starting from verse 18 where Paul speaks about Adam and death. Now, he begins to tie all of this context together. Again, remember this is a letter. The letter was written in one sitting, he did not take pauses and days to continue writing. This was their method of communication and essentially equivalent to posting onto social media.

> **[Romans 6:15-19a] What then? Shall we sin because we are not under law but under grace? Certainly not! Do you not know that to whom you present yourselves slaves to obey, you are that one's slaves whom you obey, whether of sin** *(fault, lusts, etc)* **[leading] to death, or of obedience [leading] to righteousness? But God be thanked that [though] you were** *(past tense)* **slaves of sin, yet you obeyed from the heart that form of doctrine** *(in practical terms –*

The ReDefinition of "Law" in the New Testament

> someone told you about Jesus) **to which you were delivered. And having been set free from sin, you became slaves** (not a physical slave but the giving of oneself to- submission to – you are the slave of whom you obey) **of righteousness. I speak in human [terms] because of the weakness of your flesh.**

The aforementioned scripture is powerful. The Apostle Paul tells them look because I KNOW your flesh (remember Spirit, Soul, Body) is weak – let me put aside the deep spiritual talk and tell it to you plainly. He is giving an introduction to them about how he is going to speak VERY clearly and bordering vulgar.

> **[Romans 6:19b]For just as you presented your members** (Greek word melos which can be used as a collective body however here it is referring to bodies given up to criminal intercourse, because they are as it were members belonging to the harlot's body) **[as] slaves of uncleanness, and of lawlessness [leading] to [more] lawlessness, so now present your members** (same word used as above) **[as] slaves [of] righteousness for holiness.**

In other words he tells them, the member you used as a slave to your lust with a harlot, now use it as slave to God in holiness.

> **[Romans 6:20-7:4] For when you were slaves of sin** (enslaved to whom you obeyed - lust of the flesh), **you were free** (exempt) **in regard to righteousness. What fruit did you have then in the things of which you are now ashamed?** (Those things you now feel ashamed about what fruit is there?) **For the end** (result) **of those things [is] death. But now having been set free from sin and having become slaves** (complete dedication and submission to) **of God, you have your fruit to holiness, and the end** (result)**, everlasting life. For the wages of sin [is] death, but the gift of God [is] eternal life in Christ Jesus our Lord. Or do you not know,**

> **brethren** *(for I speak to those who know the law) (in other words the Jews),* **that the law** *(Levitical law)* **has dominion over a man as long as he lives? For the woman who has a husband is bound by the law** *(Levitical AND cultural, a rule)* **to [her] husband as long as he lives. But if the husband dies, she is released from the law of [her] husband. So then if, while [her] husband lives, she marries another man, she will be called an adulteress; but if her husband dies, she is free from that law, so that she is no adulteress, though she has married another man. Therefore, my brethren** *(those who know the law – the Jews),* **you also have become dead to the law through the body of Christ, that you may be married to another - to Him who was raised from the dead, that we should bear fruit to God.**

May seem redundant but - this portion is so powerful -because he again has the context of how we are enslaved to whom we obey; there is a relationship. The word enslaved or slave is submission and dedication to. Paul continues to share this same precept under the principle or law of marriage. In the same way you were married to sin and lawlessness, and only until there is death you are released from the submission to it. Christ is the BRIDE you are the husbandman – you have to die (not physical but spiritually) so that the bride can "legally" enter into relationship – otherwise it is unlawful or adulteress. As per the law (nomos) that was the only method that a person can remarry or enter into a new covenant relationship.

> **[Romans 7:5-14] For when we were in the flesh, the sinful passions which were aroused by the law were at work in our members to bear fruit to death. But now we have been delivered** *(released from the obligation to submit to)* **from the law** *(of sin and death),* **having died to what we were held by, so that we should serve in the newness of the Spirit and not [in] the oldness of the letter. What shall we say then? [Is] the law** *(Levitical)* **sin? Certainly not! On the**

The ReDefinition of "Law" in the New Testament

contrary, I would not have known sin except through the (Levitical) law. *(Comparison and relation to commandments)* **For I would not have known covetousness unless the law had said, "You shall not covet."** *(This is in both law and commandments in Exodus 20:17 & Deuteronomy 5:21)* **But sin** *(fault)***, taking opportunity by the commandment, produced in me all [manner of evil] desire. For apart from the law sin [was] dead. I was alive once without the law, but when the commandment came, sin revived, and I died.** *(This is referring to Paul's transition from Levitical law to grace life – he was dead IN the law but then the commandment – person of Jesus)* **And the commandment** *(entole)***, which [was] to [bring] life, I found to [bring] death. For sin, taking occasion by the commandment** *(entole)***, deceived me, and by it killed [me]. Therefore, the law** *(nomos)* **[is] holy, and the commandment** *(entole)* **holy and just and good. Has then what is good become death to me?** *(in other words Paul is asking them can what is good be death to me? Can a good and just thing kill me? Can the nomos – rules or entole commandments kill me?)* **Certainly not! But sin (fault), that it might appear sin** *(a breach to the nomos or entole)***, was producing death in me through what is good, so that sin** *(a breach)* **through the commandment** *(entole)* **might become exceedingly sinful. For we know that the law** *(nomos)* **is spiritual** *(the Greek word used here does not refer to the divine spirit we ARE – but the soul where the will and the intellect reside)***, but I am carnal** *(having the nature of the flesh)***, sold under sin** *(via Adam's actions)***.**

Ok ready? Here comes the punch line to this entire study. Paul shares of his spirit – flesh struggle which I am sure each of us can relate to. Yet as we delve deeper in context, we will see something amazing. Please try to read this portion as you are speaking these words.

[Romans 7:15-24] For what I am doing *(to perform,*

accomplish, achieve), **I do not understand** *(come to know, get a knowledge or perceive)*. **For what I will to do** *(perform, accomplish, achieve)*, **that I do not** *(undertake or perform)*; **but what I hate** *(detest)*, **that I do** *(produce, as a result)*. **If, then, I do** *(produce as a result)* **what I will not to do** *(desire or love)*, **I agree** *(confess)* **the law** *(nomos)* **that [it is] good. But now** *(at this moment)*, **[it is] no longer I who do** *(produce as a result)* **it, but sin** *(the breach by Adam)* **that dwells in me** *(my soul)*. **For I know that in me** *(that is, in my flesh)* **nothing good dwells; for to will** *(the desire to produce)* **is present with me, but [how] to perform what is good I do not find** *(within my soul or flesh)*. **For** *(Greek pronoun used to introduce an explanation)* **the good** *(upright, honorable)* **that I will [to do], I do not do (produce as a result); but the evil** *(the bad nature)* **I will not [to do], that I practice (perpetuate). Now if I do what I will not [to do]** *(the evil nature)*, **it is no longer I who do it, but sin** *(the flesh)* **that dwells in me. I find then a law** *(nomos - principle)*, **that evil** *(the bad nature)* **is present with me,** *(the recognition of sin and violation of the law)* **the one who wills to do good** *(human reborn Spirit)*. **For I delight in the law of God** *(commandments)* **according to the inward man** *(human reborn spirit)*. **But I see another law** *(nomos rule, principle)* **in my members, warring against the law** *(principles)* **of my mind,** *(my soul)* **and bringing me into captivity** *(to capture one's mind)* **to the law** *(principle)* **of sin** *(a violation of the divine law in thought or in act)* **which is in my members** *(of bodies given up to criminal intercourse, because they are as it were members belonging to the harlot's body)*. **O wretched** *(afflicted)* **man** *(human being - with the adjunct notion of contempt or disdainful pity)* **that I am** *(Greek word translated for ego)*! **Who will deliver me from this body of death (the power of death and misery)?**

The ReDefinition of "Law" in the New Testament

Here comes the turn in thought and principle being shared for the growth of the church in Rome.

> **[Romans 7:25-8:1] I thank God--through Jesus Christ our Lord (Messiah)! So then, with the mind** *(renewed mind - the power of considering and judging soberly, calmly and impartially)* **I myself serve the law of God** *(commandments)*, **but with the flesh** *(the un-renewed mind)* **the law of sin** *(the breach of the commandments)*. **[There is] therefore now no condemnation** *(damnatory sentence)* **to those who are in Christ Jesus, who do not walk** *(conduct themselves in their life)* **according to the flesh** *(the earthly nature of man apart from divine influence, and therefore prone to sin and opposed to God)*, **but according to the Spirit** *(a simple essence, devoid of all or at least all grosser matter, and possessed of the power of knowing, desiring, deciding, and acting)*.

> **[Romans 8:2-9a] For the law of the Spirit of life in Christ Jesus has made me free from the law of sin and death** *(note: NOT the Law of God)*. **For what the law (nomos – rituals – Mosaic Law) could not do** *(produce by action)* **in that it was weak** *(powerless; feeble)* **through the flesh, God [did]** *(produced by action)* **by sending His own Son in the likeness** *(representation)* **of sinful flesh, on account of sin: He condemned** *(judged worthy of punishment)* **sin in the flesh, that the righteous** *(the favourable judgment by which he acquits man and declares them acceptable to Him)* **requirement of the law** *(nomos – ritual – Mosaic law)* **might be fulfilled** *(to render complete)* **in us** *(note – IN US not in CHRIST)* **who do not walk** *(regulate our life)* **according (as a standard) to the flesh but according** *(as a standard of living)* **to the Spirit** *(the disposition or influence of God in any one)*. **For those who live according to the flesh** *(sinful ways)* **set their minds on the things of the flesh** *(such as*

sin)**, but those [who live] according** *(as a standard)* **to the Spirit** *(the disposition or influence of God in anyone)***, the things of the Spirit. For to be carnally minded** *(or flesh and sin influenced)* **[is] death, but to be spiritually** *(influenced by God's wisdom)* **minded [is] life and peace. Because the carnal mind** *(flesh and sin influence)* **[is] enmity against God; for it is not subject to the law of God** *(not Mosaic but 10 Commandments)***, nor indeed can be. So then, those who are in the flesh cannot please God.** *(The context of this statement is that one who is NOT influenced by the Spirit of God and the 10 Commandments – God's Law- cannot please God)***. But you are not in the flesh (sinful nature) but in the Spirit** *(influence of God)***, if indeed the Spirit of God dwells in you.**

Paul ends this discourse with more to follow, yet the summation of the context is clear. He tells them, BUT you are not in the flesh, so as you walk out God's Law not in the flesh which is dead but in the spirit-reborn, righteous state - **you please the Father**.

Our disdain with the Ten Commandments has placed us in a place where we are not pleasing the Father. There is only one other place where it gives us CLEAR context of how to "please" the Father- For it is impossible to please God without faith.

This faith is the act of believing what He says is true, is integral, and necessary for our walk in the Spirit. It is the relationship of Love that will include a spirit lead life based on love and yes, a moral standard of not operating in the flesh – outside of God's law. Again, not Mosaic law – GOD'S LAW. Furthermore, without the Ten Commandments (God's Law) there is no violation or a transgression; without one there is no sin of which we know very well there is. If we eliminate sin then we must also eliminate its counterpart – temptation and to say there is no temptation because the Ten Commandments are nullified is wrong.

Upon the current foundation we have established in our study of the first part of Romans we can now enter in more understanding of this glorious letter written about the Grace of God toward us.

> **[Romans 13:8-15 NKJV] Owe no man any thing, but to love one another: for he that loveth** *(his fellow brother/sister)* **another hath fulfilled** *(completed; fulfill; consummate)* **the** *(nomos)* **law.** *(The word nomos is used there however it is both God's law and Mosaic Law sue to the audience being spoken to; if we continue to read we will see the following:)* **For this, Thou shalt not commit adultery , Thou shalt not kill , Thou shalt not steal , Thou shalt not bear false witness , Thou shalt not covet ; and if there be any other commandment, it is briefly comprehended in this saying, namely, Thou shalt love thy neighbour as thyself. Love worketh no ill to his neighbour: therefore love is the fulfilling** *(verb tense of fulfilled - completed; fulfill; consummate)* **of the law** *(nomos, Ten Commandments as context reveals)*.

With this in mind we must revisit the thought pattern that we cannot fulfill the law. That the Ten Commandments are no longer in play, and how this cannot be right. The reason is, if Paul is calling the Romans to exemplify LOVE via the observance of the Ten Commandments, then we must be able to not only fulfill it but even be required to fulfill it in our walk. In fact when we do not, this would be a transgression and a requirement for repentance – which is where GRACE is available to you. Paul is not saying how Christ did it, but how we are to.

We can see clearly when Jesus speaks multiple times in John that what Paul was referencing in this scripture was the Ten Commandments.

> **[John 13:34 KJV] A new commandment** *(entole)* **I give unto you, That ye love one another; as I have loved you, that ye also love one another.**
>
> **[John 14:15 KJV] If ye love me, keep my commandments.** *(entole)*

A Balanced Life

> [John 14:21 KJV] - He that hath my commandments, *(entole)* and keepeth them, he it is that loveth me: and he that loveth me shall be loved of my Father, and I will love him, and will manifest myself to him.

In John 14:21 Jesus speaking says in context – those who love me keep His commandments, and in keeping them is indicative of the love we have for Him. Via that love is how God love's us, and how CHRIST will manifest Himself to us through what we know of as GRACE!

> [John 15:10 KJV] - If ye keep my commandments, *(entole)* ye shall abide in my love; even as I have kept my father's commandments, *(entole)* and abide in his love.

> [John 15:12 KJV] - This is my commandment, *(entole)* That ye love one another, as I have loved you.

This is why the fulcrum to our scale is the Person of Love. If He is in Love (the Father) keeping His commandments *(entole)*, then we must also be in Love (the Father) and keep His commandments *(entole)*. Not the Law of Moses (this is not what is being said here) but the commandments of the FATHER (the Law of God) which was given to Abraham sometime before Genesis 26:5 (revert to chapter 1&2).

> [John 14:9-18] "Jesus saith unto him, Have I been so long time with you, and yet hast thou not known me, Philip? he that hath seen me hath seen the Father; and how sayest thou then, Shew us the Father? Believest thou not that I am in the Father, and the Father in me? the words that I speak unto you I speak not of myself: but the Father that dwelleth in me, he doeth the works. Believe me that I am in the Father, and the Father in me: or else believe me for the very works' sake. Verily, verily, I say unto you, He that believeth on me, the works that I do shall he do also; and greater works than these shall he do; because I go unto my Father. And whatsoever ye shall ask in my name, that will I do, that the Father may be glorified in the Son. If ye shall

The ReDefinition of "Law" in the New Testament

ask any thing in my name, I will do it. If ye love me, keep my commandments *(entole)*. And I will pray the Father, and he shall give you another Comforter, that he may abide with you for ever; Even the Spirit of truth; whom the world cannot receive, because it seeth him not, neither knoweth him: but ye know him; for he dwelleth with you and shall be in you. I will not leave you comfortless: I will come to you." *(Again – RELATIONSHIP)*

So with the understanding that the Father is IN Him and He in the Father when Jesus says, if you love me keep my commandments it is as if the Father is saying it.

Not only that, but get this – receiving the Comforter is based upon the requirement of loving Him and Keeping His commandments *(entole)*. In the above scripture Jesus, just like God, gives conditional requirements.

- **He that believes on me and the works that I do – shall he also do.** *(Belief is the foundation of our faith – if we do not believe what He has done – how can we fathom that we would be able to as well?)*

- **If you ask anything in my name, I will do it.** *(To ask is the acknowledgement of humility, and need)*

- **If you love me and keep my commandments; Father will give you a comforter.** *(An act of grace to balance the scale)*

One of the most powerful examples of this and someone now having a balanced scale is found in the book of Mark. The subtitle is the "rich young ruler" and the scenario is a young leader who is financially prosperous but emotionally poor *(read my book Prosperity Delusion for more details)* he is asking Jesus to be a part of the "team".

> **[Mark 10:17-22] says the following; "And when he was gone forth into the way, there came one running, and kneeled to him, and asked him, Good Master, what shall I do that I may inherit eternal life? And Jesus said unto him, why**

A Balanced Life

callest thou me good? there is none good but one, that is, God. Thou knowest the commandments *(entole)*, **Do not commit adultery, Do not kill, Do not steal, Do not bear false witness, Defraud not, Honour thy father and mother. And he answered and said unto him, Master, <u>all these have I observed from my youth.</u> Then Jesus beholding him loved him,** *(fulfilling the words he spoke – those who love me keep my commandments and I will love them)* **and said unto him, One thing thou lackest: go thy way, sell whatsoever thou hast, and give to the poor, and thou shalt have treasure in heaven: and come, take up the cross, and follow me. And he was sad at that saying, and went away grieved: for he had great possessions."**

I want to outline 2 very specific things which occurred here:

1. Notice that Christ did not call him a LIAR! He did not tell this young man, "You have not kept the commandments - it is impossible for you to keep the commandments only I can". This tells us that it can be accomplished and is a valid requirement. And unlike the woman at the well – Jesus did not confront him on this matter.

Then it says that Christ Loved him (relationship) and He tells him "ONE THING you lack - sell all that you have". The primary reason Jesus told him that was because his act of love had to be demonstrated. He observed the *entole* (commandments) but never demonstrated the position of relationship nor the love that the observance of them should yield. Essentially he probably did not live in a grace-based life.

Observance of the Ten Commandments should always yield or produce LOVE, not the other way around. LOVE does not produce as a result the observance of the Ten Commandments. Remember if you LOVE me – keep my commandments. The "if" preceeds the result of the condition.

When His disciples asked about this, what was His reply? It was a clear and concise response: **"there is no one who has left mother or father ...for MY SAKE and the gospels"** (verse 29) shall have eternal life.

2. The other part we must learn from this is that Jesus gave the requirement to the question, what must one do to inherit eternal life? Not only that but Jesus tells the rich young ruler if you can do that – once you do it, come and follow me.

It is EXTREMELY important to note that I am not advocating that we must satisfy the 10 Commandments to be saved! I submit that when God brings this all-full circle because the Law existed way before Moses presented it, then it should be a moral standard (the Ten Commandments) for the believer.

The New Testament says, that it is written in our hearts no longer on stone. The context of that message is that for a believer it is written in the heart; what is? The Ten Commandments; The Law of Love.

For God is Love and therefore God's Law is the Law of LOVE.

War a good warfare, why? Because these temptations will come, they will arrive when you least expect, however standing firm in the LAW of LOVE allows you to overcome the temptation through the acknowledgment and repentance of a transgression. If there is no acknowledgment, then you continue as if all is well but it is not.

Most people look at this and focus on what you cannot do. We must stop doing this, this is liberating. That is why most people have issues with this. They look at it as - I can't do this and I can't do that. No look at it through the eyes of Love; I will not kill someone because my God loves them no matter what they do. I will not have a graven image because my God is jealous, and I love Him. I will not covet my neighbors' belongings because I love my neighbor as I do myself. It is a choice of Love manifested through Grace. Essentially becoming BOTH/AND and not EITHER/OR.

Grace without LAW allows for no restraint and becomes a license to sin or a lawless life of which is spoken of in the aforementioned text.

How is it in one breath we can say the mind is the battlefield and yet the other breath say that grace will not allow you to do it?

A Balanced Life

[Ephesians 4:17-32] This I say therefore, and testify in the Lord, that ye henceforth walk not as other Gentiles walk, in the vanity of their mind, Having the understanding darkened, being alienated from the life of God through the ignorance that is in them, because of the blindness of their heart: Who being past feeling have given themselves over unto lasciviousness, to work all uncleanness with greediness. But ye have not so learned Christ; If so be that ye have heard him, and have been taught by him, as the truth is in Jesus: That ye put off concerning the former conversation the old man, which is corrupt according to the deceitful lusts; And be renewed in the spirit of your mind; And that ye put on the new man, which after God is created in righteousness and true holiness. Wherefore putting away lying, speak every man truth with his neighbour: for we are members one of another. Be ye angry, and sin not: let not the sun go down upon your wrath: Neither give place to the devil. Let him that stole steal no more: but rather let him labour, working with his hands the thing which is good, that he may have to give to him that needeth. Let no corrupt communication proceed out of your mouth, but that which is good to the use of edifying, that it may minister grace unto the hearers. And grieve not the holy Spirit of God, whereby ye are sealed unto the day of redemption. Let all bitterness, and wrath, and anger, and clamor, and evil speaking, be put away from you, with all malice: And be ye kind one to another, tenderhearted, forgiving one another, even as God for Christ's sake hath forgiven you.

Verse 23 renew your mind. Renew your method of thinking.

If grace was sufficient then why would Paul admonish the people to repent from sin? Not only Paul, look at 1 Peter 2:11 and 2 Peter 2:8 which says: **"For that righteous man dwelling among them, in seeing**

and hearing, vexed his righteous soul from day to day with their unlawful deeds." UNLAWFUL DEEDS RIGHTEOUS SOUL.. Here you have a righteous soul committing unlawful deeds. A believer violating the commandments.

Again I close with this one true fact - This is not a salvation issue. I believe that the Ten Commandments is a moral standard defined by our Creator to know how to live right and identity wrong and repent. Otherwise without it we have no idea how to love, we have no idea how to worship and we have no idea how to be in relationship. Without the counterbalance there is no need for grace. There is **A LAW** which God asks of us to fulfill. It was not first given to Moses in Exodus it was given WAY before as we see from Genesis 26:5. Abraham knew them and to the point that he kept them - ae are Abraham's seed just like Isaac was. The young rich ruler kept them which tells us they are not impossible to keep.

We can see the example GOD gave us in creation:

"You shall have no other God's before me." Adam and Eve allowed the serpent to beguile them. This is not just the obvious deception but for that moment they allowed the serpent to be their god.

"Remember the Sabbath day and keep it Holy." 6 days work – 1 day rest in creation.

"Honor your father and mother." If this was not communicated then why would the rebellion of Adam and Eve have any consequence. Obedience is Honor.

"Thou shalt not kill." If the standard was not defined then why would Cain killing Able be an issue?

"Thou shalt not steal." Was Eve's transgression by taking the fruit of the tree that was off limits – an act of theft? Yes! If this was not clarified as a standard, why would this be an issue?

These are rhetorical questions for you to begin to change the paradigm, and mindset concerning the commandments.

A Balanced Life

Are any of these really a hard request from the Father? Honestly? Why do so many defend the right to kill someone, commit adultery, steal, have other gods. Ok maybe not defend it, but most assuredly claim that the 10 Commandments are unfulfillable and nullified by Christ – which is incorrect. We must tear down the idol of grace we have built and replace it with a scale, a balance, a plumb line of which we measure ourselves via the renewing of our mind.

Jesus was sent to be the gift for the collective redemption of a people when we look through the lenses of the priestly duties, the tabernacle, the Mosaic law and the Levitical law. When it comes to God's law (10 Commandments) grace which was always there before Christ (seen in Abraham, Moses) God steps in to redeem or declare righteous. Then we approach the person of Love and God provided the method to come to the person of Love (Himself – God is Love) by way of His son.

The largest challenge for many is that the primary word for SIN in the Old Testament is translated to mean punishment. Yet in the New Testament it is translated mostly to "miss the mark". Giving the word picture of an archery target, the lines from the center out are titled Sin 1, Sin2, Sin 3 respectively. Consider for a moment the target being "salvation". Which is an act of grace. You hit the "target" all the time as a blood washed Christian since you accepted Jesus as Savior. Yet in your walk you hit the "target" but miss the dead center and hit "sin1 or Sin2". The Love God has for you and you for Him, calls you back and through grace gets you to hit dead center again. It is like grace takes the arrow - you shot - pulls it out and puts it dead center again - WHEN we repent of missing the mark. An act of Love by God to bring you BACK into right standing again.

Moments to Ponder:

Take the time to read Romans without chapters and verses after completing this chapter. (Tip: even if you need to go to the website Blueletterbible.com and download it and put it into a word document - I challenge you to do it!)

A Picture of the Balanced Life

So what does a "Balanced Life" look like? How do we put shoe leather to what is shared in this book? What is it that we need to implement in our lives to help us have Love as our fulcrum and commandment and grace on their perspective sides of the scale?

I will not sugar coat this and tell you it will be easy. However, know that it is VERY attainable. It is through Christ who gives us the ability to cry "Abba Father".

For me the best way to maintain a balanced life is to have a heart of repentance. Having a heart of repentance allows grace to flow and accountability to the commandments at the same time. Paul in his writing to the church in Corinth reminds them that these things are an example.

> [1 Cor. 10:6-11 NKJV] Now these things became our examples, to the intent that we should not lust after evil things as they also lusted. And do not become idolaters as [were] some of them. As it is written, "The people sat

> **down to eat and drink, and rose up to play." Nor let us commit sexual immorality, as some of them did, and in one day twenty-three thousand fell; nor let us tempt Christ, as some of them also tempted, and were destroyed by serpents; nor complain, as some of them also complained, and were destroyed by the destroyer. Now all these things happened to them as examples, and they were written for our admonition, upon whom the ends of the ages have come.**

When we are challenged or tempted in a particular way, the knowledge of what is the law of Love will give a "check" to our spirit man and let us know it is wrong. We then allow grace to step in and balance the scale because grace will let us know, "I am here for you and I am going to tip the scale so that you can make the RIGHT decision and have LOVE as your center"; the person of Love is your central focus. The result being, I will not do this because I do not want to offend the One who Loves me.

This is where we get in Romans 5:20 **"Moreover the law entered, that the offence might abound. But where sin abounded, grace did much more abound."** He was referencing the Old Testament patriarchs."

Grace will always tip the scale because its "mass" is greater than that of sin. Yet without the knowledge of sin there is no reciprocal.

In a covenant of marriage, we exercise this time and time again or perhaps for some quite often. Temptation arises, we know that what can be done is wrong, yet grace steps in and says, don't offend the one you love.

It is not solely a don't do this or that, it is the perspective of living a life where the reality of temptation is there however the scale will be tipped on your way to help you make the RIGHT decision. Yet the decision will continue and will always be yours (that pesky freewill thing) – you choose this day.

[James 4:6] He gives grace to the humble.

This leads us to assume what the proud lack. The proud do not have an understanding of the reciprocal, so they will constantly fall to temptations. Remember Pride comes before the fall. The most greatest act of humility is not washing feet, or serving others, it is the ability to recognize that you cant do this faith walk alone. That your need for Him is much greater than His need for you.

[Esther 2:17] *Lets us know that doing the "right thing" results in when it says:* **And the king loved Esther above all the women, and she obtained grace and favor in his sight more than all the virgins; so that he set the royal crown upon her head, and made her queen instead of Vashti.**

This gives us a depiction of the result of a balanced life. Esther is one example of a balanced life – perfect? NO! Humble? YES! It was this humility and heart of repentance that placed her as queen when someone else was "supposed" to be there.

When we live a balanced life, doors swing open and things happen that violate the worldly standard because grace and favor is upon you. A person who understands the scale, that when there is a transgression in the commandment, there is repentance through the person of Love and grace is made available, will be a person who is successful and would seem like "things" just happen for them.

It is time for us as a church people to return to this so that we are no longer considered hypocrites, but people who love. People who love God and people and truly see that every person has a good in them but just need to learn how the balance works. Share it with them.

It is this that resembles a grace-based life in balance.

Dr. Marc Garcia – Biography:

Dr. Marc Garcia a family man, a US Navy veteran, and an ordained minister with a passion for leadership. He earned his Doctorate in Biblical Studies from the North Carolina College of Theology in 2006 and has had the opportunity to train in both the church and business sectors. He has embraced Ecclesiates 1:13 as a cornerstone scripture, which says:

> **And I have given my heart to seek and to search out by wisdom concerning all that hath been done under the heavens. It is a challenging task God has given to the sons of man to be humbled by it.**

Dr. Marc is drawn to equipping people, especially leaders. Everything he does is to encourage others in their God-given pursuit of the One who has called each of us unto Himself. He has had the honor to do this through his time in radio, television and books. He has a heart for transparency and building strong foundations.

Dr. Marc and his wife, Blanca, have been married for over 20 years, raised a son, and are also licensed foster parents. They have written numerous books and together have forged not only their own relationship with Christ in the middle but also their individual relationship with Him. They currently reside in South Carolina and you can find their content, podcasts and programs online.

Ministry: https://BeTheBridgeSC.org
Business: https://www.nuevavida.media

Empowering You Podcast:
https://podcasters.spotify.com/pod/show/empoweryou-drmarc

Other Writings available by
Dr. Marc Garcia & Blanca Garcia

An insightful, empowering (not critical) look at the "prosperity gospel" that will shake the foundation. Our frame of believing has been conditioned to either embrace it or despise it with a passion. So what does true prosperity look like? When it comes down to "shoe leather walking out faith" what is prosperity? Does it look like cars, houses, bank accounts? Come and discover and perhaps redefine what prosperity is. Let's re-frame some delusions concerning this "prosperity gospel". Are you ready?

Two words that not only impacted the lives of 12 but impacted the world for centuries. In this insightful book Dr Marc Garcia delves into the depths to give us a clear understanding as to why these two words - Follow Me - not only caused successful men to leave what they where doing but has impacted the lives of many throughout history.

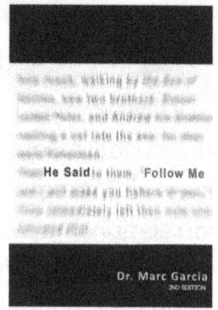

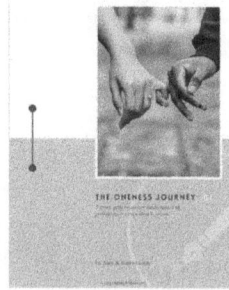

After 15 years of annually retreating, Dr. Marc and Blanca Garcia have taken from their experience and developed this retreat workbook to help marriages re-inforce their unity and oneness. This workbook is part of a series where this is the "101" version and there is another edition for ministerial leaders. (201)

Other Writings available by Dr. Marc Garcia & Blanca Garcia

Is life messy right now? Are you facing an unplanned pregnancy? Do you fear what the future holds? You are not alone. Motherhood is hard on all new moms, especially when they happen to be a teenager. While your friends are making decisions about college and which movie to go see on Friday night, your attention is being pulled in another direction.Whether you choose to keep your baby or give another family hope through the blessing of adoption, you are about to experience a level of sacrifice you have never known before. Unplanned is here so that you'll give yourself a chance. Even with a child on your hip, you can still give yourself the opportunity to pursue the God-given dreams that are tucked away in your heart. Do not allow the circumstances to talk you out of the powerful future that is still ahead of you.Blanca shares her moving story so that you will learn from her choices and laugh along with her awkward moments. With hope as a main theme woven throughout, Unplanned leads you as a teen-mom, to reflect on heartfelt questions. The fact is, you can make it. There will be tears, but it will be worth it. Your life is not over, it is just going to be different than you

www.ingramcontent.com/pod-product-compliance
Lightning Source LLC
Chambersburg PA
CBHW060213050426
42446CB00013B/3064